The Right Jewelry For You

How to select and wear jewelry that suits your features, personality, and budget

by
James Avery
with Karen Jackson

Eakin Press ☆ Austin, Texas

FIRST EDITION

Copyright © 1988
By James Avery Craftsman, Inc.

Published in the United States of America
By Eakin Publications, Inc.
P.O. Box 23069, Austin, Texas 78735

ISBN 0-89015-654-9

Book Design: Sue Heatly Associates, Austin, Texas
Cover Photo: Tomás Pantin
Illustrations: George Strickland, John Wilson

LIBRARY OF CONGRESS
Library of Congress Cataloging-in-Publication Data

Avery, James. 1921–
   The right jewelry for you : how to select and wear the jewelry that suits your features, personality, and budget / James Avery with Karen Jackson.
      p.   cm.
   ISBN 0-89015-654-9
   1. Jewelry—Purchasing. 2. Beauty, Personal. I. Jackson, Karen, 1945–
II. Title.
TS729.A94 1988
646–dc19   88-16035
                                                              CIP

Acknowledgments

To those who have given of their time and talents to make this idea become a reality goes a special word of thanks: to Mike McIntyre for his initial concept and his untiring efforts to see it to completion; and to Leslie Nichols, Pat Thalken, and Shirley Kitzman for their ideas, enthusiasm, and judicious editing.

Contents

Introduction

Ever since I was a small boy I have enjoyed making things and working with my hands, fitting and joining materials together in the finest way I knew how. So it was very simple and most enjoyable for me in 1954, when I started making jewelry in a garage, to sit down and sketch out an idea, then proceed to create. It was this same simple enjoyment that I wanted to share with others.

Back in those days, working alone, I could meet each individual customer and discuss her needs. With this kind of one-on-one relationship, discovering each woman's needs was simple — as was seeing which pieces of jewelry brought out her special individualism, personality, and features. In my small shop it was easy to find out what a woman wanted to accomplish with her jewelry and then to offer suggestions to help her achieve those desired results.

But in three decades, we've grown. Instead of one small shop, we now have many retail stores, hundreds of dealerships nationwide, and thousands of mail-order customers. And although I'm grateful for this growth, maintaining close relationships with customers and offering them specific help has become difficult. For this very reason, in trying to help women wear jewelry more attractively and effectively, we decided to write this book.

It is certainly true that women are becoming more and more aware of their image and what jewelry can do for that image. If anything, this awareness is more defined than it was when I began. And although many books have been written to provide guidelines for women to wear clothes, hairstyles, and cosmetics to their best advantage, none on wearing jewelry to that same advantage has been written until now.

This book is an attempt to reach any of you who want to learn the art of wearing jewelry well. It is my hope that this book helps rather than dictates; that it encourages rather than deters. In order that the book have fundamental principles and longevity, we have illustrated it with jewelry that is representative of universal styles and not the work of any one manufacturer or designer. After you've read it, I hope that it will be "your reference book" on the buying and wearing of jewelry.

For when understood, jewelry can be a fun, creative way to project an image that's all you.

James Avery

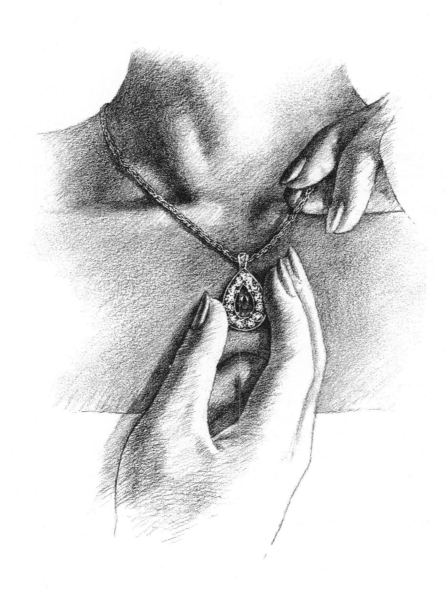

Part
I

Wearing the Right Jewelry

1 *Exploring New Beginnings*

You're almost ready to step out for a very special occasion. A job interview, a first date, lunch with the mayor, a PTA board meeting, a romantic, candlelight dinner.

You've chosen the perfect outfit—one that looks good on you and says what you want to say about yourself. A final check in the mirror assures you that your hair and make-up look just right.

Then you turn to your jewelry box.

What pieces will you choose to wear for this special occasion? How much should you wear? Which are the right colors? What shapes will flatter? What jewelry styles will carry through the well thought-out image you want to project?

As you peer into your jewelry box, some possibilities catch your eye. Maybe this is the occasion to wear that newest addition to your jewelry collection—the gemstone ring and matching pendant you have just received as a gift. The pair is so noticeable and eye-catching. But, on the other hand, they may seem a little *too* flashy. And today of all days is not a time to be plagued by "appearance worry."

So you look for other "safer" pieces. Still, your uncertainty about choosing jewelry shadows every selection. The silver pieces seem too bold, the costume jewelry too casual. The gold hoop earrings have never flattered you. The gold filled chain looks promising, but you remember that the thin outer layer of gold has worn through in several spots — reminding you again of one of the mistakes you've made in buying jewelry because you didn't understand what you were getting.

One by one, you consider and then discard pieces of your collection. Within a few short moments all those shiny objects have succeeded in becoming obstacles to effective dressing rather than giving the final polish to your perfect outfit.

So, in the end, you reach for the old tried-and-true pieces you always seem to wear. As you leave, you wonder if there isn't a way to gain more satisfaction and less frustration from owning and wearing jewelry.

But how?

It's time, you realize, to find out about jewelry — how to buy it as an informed consumer, how to wear the right pieces at the right times, and how you can use it to bring out the best in you.

Jewelry: the word comes from the French word *joiel*, which means "joy." On the one hand, jewelry can be fascinating and enhancing, a source of pleasure and exciting adornment. But for many women, as the opening scenario points out, jewelry can be a source of uncertainty, frustration, and even intimidation.

This book was written to help you buy and wear your jewelry with "joy" and with confidence — whether it's rubies or rhinestones, platinum or plastic, simple earrings or multiple strands of pearls. It is a collection of practical guidelines, observations, tips, suggestions, and techniques you can use to buy any jewelry with confidence and then wear it well, excitingly well. You'll become familiar with the basic essentials, then learn to choose your jewelry so that it makes a positive contribution to your wardrobe, appearance, and self-confidence.

THE BEGINNING

The first step in learning how to determine the right jewelry for you lies in self-evaluation. The following questions are designed to help you evaluate your strengths as well as point to any weaknesses you might have when it comes to jewelry. It takes only a few minutes and there are no wrong or right answers — only self-enlightenment and insight.

Your Jewelry and You: A Test

Answer each of the following questions by checking the answer that best describes you or your present jewelry collection.

Yes   No   Sometimes

☐   ☐   ☐   1. Do you receive compliments on the jewelry you wear?

☐   ☐   ☐   2. Do you buy your jewelry with the same confidence you do your clothes, furniture, or a television set?

Yes   No   Sometimes

☐   ☐   ☐   3. Are you often asked where you bought a piece of your jewelry?

☐   ☐   ☐   4. If you had a job interview this morning, a Broadway opening tonight, a picnic tomorrow afternoon, and a romantic dinner planned for this weekend, could your jewelry collection meet the different demands of these occasions?

☐   ☐   ☐   5. When you buy a new clothing outfit, do you consider how jewelry might complete it?

☐   ☐   ☐   6. Do you rarely buy "mistakes"—pieces you don't wear after you get them home because, for one reason or another, they don't look or feel right?

☐   ☐   ☐   7. Do you know how to care for your jewelry so it will look good while you wear it, and also last long enough to pass on to your daughter?

☐   ☐   ☐   8. Do you consider your lifestyle when you choose your jewelry?

☐   ☐   ☐   9. When it comes to buying jewelry—from costume to fine—do you know what qualities and characteristics to look for as well as what to look *out* for?

Yes   No   Sometimes

☐   ☐   ☐   10. Do you know how the quality of
                       precious metals is measured — how
                       much pure gold is in 14-karat gold,
                       how much pure silver is in sterling
                       silver?

☐   ☐   ☐   11. Do you wish you knew more about
                       gemstones?

SCORING

_____ Yes

_____ No

_____ Sometimes

Give yourself two points for every answer of "yes,"
one point for every answer of "sometimes," and zero
points for an answer of "no." Then add your points. If
the total is eighteen or more, you positively gleam when
it comes to jewelry. If it ranges between thirteen and
eighteen, then your effectiveness could use a little
polishing. Twelve or under and you're not alone, but
you probably could use some help in buying and wearing
jewelry. Read on.

 *Starting at the Top*

What's the first thing you notice when you look at someone? Their face?

Most likely. It's the first part of your body most people notice. It's also where their eyes stay the longest. In fact, studies indicate that as much as 90 percent of a person's interest centers on your face.

Faces have played a decisive role throughout history. Helen of Troy was said to have had a face so beautiful it launched a thousand ships in a war between the Greeks and the Trojans to decide who would possess her. Anne of Cleves, on the other hand, was said to have had a face so displeasing that Henry VIII banished her from his court after only one glance. In fact, the king was so appalled by her homeliness that he had their marriage, which had been performed by proxy, annulled and the minister who had negotiated it beheaded!

For an idea of just how much attention centers on your face, try this experiment. Watch the next two or three people you meet and make a mental note of how long they look at your face. Then compare that to the time they look elsewhere — at your hands, your hair, or your clothes. The results will probably surprise you.

With all of this attention directed toward your face, the jewelry you wear near it (earrings, necklaces, pins) should be given primary consideration. These small accessories contribute in a big way to your overall image and appearance. Except for a hat, scarf, or eyeglasses, jewelry is the only "clothing" there is to enhance your facial features. Choosing those pieces that complement and enhance your face is, therefore, one of the first steps in learning to wear the best jewelry for you.

Fortunately, it is also one of the easiest.

INTERACTION

Three factors influence the jewelry that flatters your face:

1) The shape of your face
2) The shape of your jewelry
3) How these two shapes interact.

Every woman has inherited one of the four basic facial shapes: oval, round, square, or heart-shaped. It's impossible for all earrings and all necklaces to look good on all women. Your jewelry works best when you use it to harmonize with your special facial shape. Determining which pieces those are depends on three factors: the shape of your face, the shape of your jewelry, and how these two combine or *interact*.

Before determining your special facial shape and finding the pieces that bring out the best of that shape, it helps to understand first how interaction works. To start with, consider the example of two sisters with two very different facial shapes. They are Shirley and Elaine.

Of the four types of faces, Shirley's is round. For a cocktail party tonight, Shirley is wearing a pair of circular, button-type earrings set with large round pearls. To these she has added a wide, choker-length necklace of many strands of seed pearls.

Her sister, Elaine, has a very different facial shape. Hers is heart-shaped and comes to a distinct point at the chin. To the same cocktail party her sister is attending, Elaine wears a pair of 3″ drop-style earrings and a matching pendant worn on a long chain.

Take just a moment to consider the shape of these women's faces when they combine or *interact* with the jewelry they are wearing.

Shirley   Elaine

Before
The wrong combination of jewelry and facial shape can actually detract from your appearance.

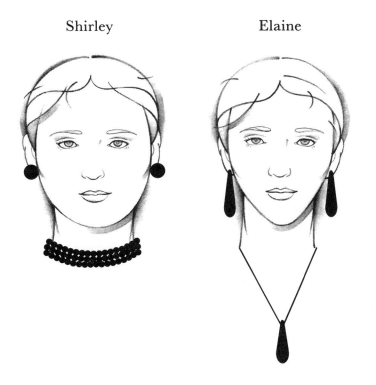

Are these the best pieces of jewelry that the two women could have chosen to wear? What would happen if the sisters exchanged their jewelry before attending the cocktail party?

After

The jewelry now works to bring out the best in the different facial shapes.

Shirley   Elaine

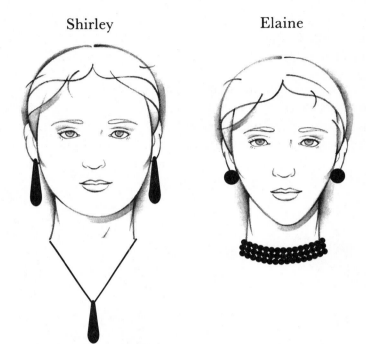

Now the jewelry interacts positively with the faces of each woman — complementing, enhancing, flattering.

But why?

When you select jewelry, or any other clothing item, you put two or more things together to achieve a certain effect. In doing this, one of three things can happen.

The first is negative, as it was when Shirley and Elaine first chose their jewelry. Compare the appearance of the two women before and after they exchanged jewelry. Notice that in the first instance, the shape of the jewelry actually detracted from their appearance.

The second outcome is a positive one. Two shapes can interact in a way that improves and enhances your appearance. This is what happened after the sisters exchanged their jewelry. The shape of the jewelry worked with the shape of their faces to create a more flattering appearance.

A third possibility is that the interaction is neither positive nor negative, and therefore, neither improves nor detracts. However, because you are working to have your jewelry enhance your appearance, this possibility is, in a way, a negative one for you.

Positive interaction—the unique ability of shapes to interact to flatter—is one of the key powers of jewelry. The five basic design principles that follow will help you determine the jewelry that will do the most for you. These principles can be used as guidelines to help you choose the jewelry that enhances you.

Lines

The first three principles are concerned with the lines of the jewelry you wear. Look at the examples on the next page. Notice that lines are very effective in directing eye movement. In the world of fashion, the ability to use lines to direct eye movement in a desired manner is essential. It allows you to visually alter your appearance by seeming taller or shorter, broader or thinner.

Remembering the following three principles will help you use the lines of your jewelry to your advantage:

> *Horizontal lines broaden and shorten*
> *Vertical lines slim and elongate*
> *Diagonal line slim and elongate*

Squinting your eyes can sometimes help you see the predominant direction, vertical or horizontal, of a piece.

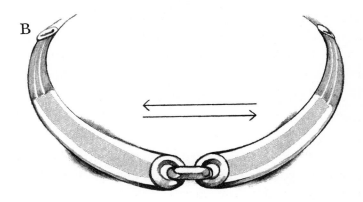

Notice that the predominant line of a piece of jewelry can actually be a part of the design, as they are in the earrings in example A, or they can be the principal silhouette of the piece as in the choker in example B. Often simply squinting your eyes can help you see the principal direction of a piece.

The jewelry that Elaine first wore featured strong vertical lines which slimmed and elongated a face that was already long and thinned a chin that was already thin. When she switched, however, the strong horizontal lines of the pearl, button-type earrings and the choker visually shortened and broadened her face. The interaction of her jewelry with her face shape produced pleasing results.

There is a final factor to keep in mind when beginning to work with the lines of your jewelry. Because lines lead the eye in a certain direction, they can be used very effectively to direct the eye *to* or *away* from a special feature.

When selecting your jewelry, a major concern is the direction of the lines of the piece.

Repetition

Repetition is simply repeating something frequently to reinforce and emphasize it. Repetition can be used to accentuate pattern, shape, color, or style. It works much like the da-da-da-dum theme of Beethoven's Fifth Symphony. This theme, repeated many times throughout the work, becomes the dominant idea of the entire piece of music.

There is only one principle concerning repetition and the choice of your jewelry:

> *Because repetition emphasizes, never at something you do not want to emphasize*

You can see how the circular earrings Shirley first chose repeated and emphasized the roundness of her face. When she exchanged earrings, the vertical lines of the new pair interacted pleasingly with her round face instead of emphasizing its roundness.

Proportion

Proportion is how one object is viewed relative to a second object. It is basically a comparison. For example, if you are a woman measuring 5'10", you are considered tall by everyday standards. But, if the starting line-up of the Boston Celtics trots up and surrounds you, you appear less tall, maybe even short!

People are accustomed to what they perceive as "normal" or "typical" proportions. If you wear jewelry that is either oversized or diminutive for your body size, people interpret the jewelry as out of proportion or out of harmony with the norm. When this happens, your jewelry will either draw all the attention or be so insignificant that it has no impact.

*In general, jewelry will be most complementary
when it is in proportion to your height and build*

The principles of lines, repetition, and proportion are not indicators of "good" or "bad." They are simply rules that have proven beneficial over time. The guidelines don't have to limit your freedom or ability to have fun when choosing and wearing your jewelry. They are merely starting points, allowing you to focus your jewelry selections on those pieces that flatter you. And they allow you to make your choices with confidence.

TRADITIONAL NAMES OF NECKLACES

Name	Length	Name	Length
Choker	14″ – 16″	Opera	28″ – 30″
Princess	18″	Rope	longer than 40″
Matinée	20″ – 24″		

BASIC FACIAL SHAPES

Now comes the fun part — putting what you've learned about interaction to work with the special shape of your face. Although no woman's face is like any other, there are four basic facial shapes: round, heart-shaped, square, and oval.

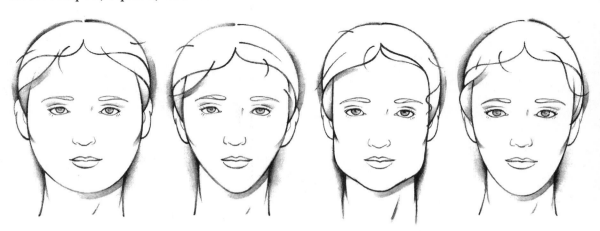

Round   Heart-shaped   Square   Oval

How to Find Your Facial Shape

Oval, round, heart-shaped, or square: which of these shapes does your face most closely approximate? If you don't know, there are a couple of quick, simple ways to help you find out. One is to tie your hair back with a ribbon. Then close one eye and trace the outline of your face in the bathroom mirror with a bar of soap. Step back and look at the shape you've drawn. It should be close to an oval, circle, square, or heart.

Another way to find the shape of your face (less messy, although not quite as accurate) is to hold a long pencil vertically at the corner of one eye. The outline of your face extending beyond the pencil should indicate the general shape of your face.

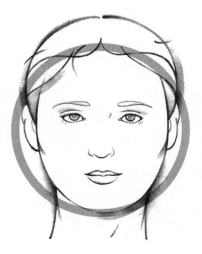

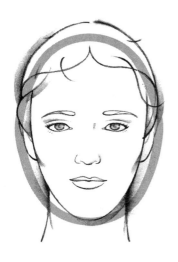

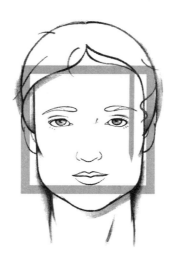

One way to find your facial shape is to hold a pencil at the corner of your eye. The shape extending outside the pencil should give you an indication of which basic shape is yours.

Of course, few people have a perfectly oval, round, square, or heart-shaped face. Almost everyone, however, does tend toward one of these shapes.

Of these four basic shapes, an oval face is considered to be the "perfect" shape for today's American woman. Times change, however, and so do people's ideas of what is perfect. Different eras have idealized different kinds of women. In nineteenth-century Victorian novels, most heroines had "perfect," heart-shaped faces. The "perfect" models of Rubens had round, fleshier ones. Today, the modern ideal favors a face that's an oval.

If your face isn't oval, don't despair. Bringing out the best in yours takes little more than a good eye and applying the principles concerning lines, repetition, and proportion.

YOUR FACE AND YOUR JEWELRY

The Oval Face

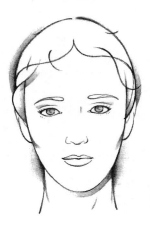

Women with oval faces can wear any shape of jewelry.

If you've found your facial shape is oval, lucky you. Women with this shape face have few restrictions on the jewelry they wear around their face. Any shape earring works well—from buttons to hoops or dangling drops—as well as any type or length of necklace. You can wear a choker of small pearls or a rope of large silver beads with equal ease and effect. If this is your facial shape, your only limitations are those of proportion. It's important to scale the size of your earrings and necklace to the size of your face and body.

If your oval face is slightly long, button-shaped earrings or round hoops can help increase the appearance of width. You can also give the illusion of width by wearing a shorter necklace, such as a choker or princess-length necklace.

The Square Face

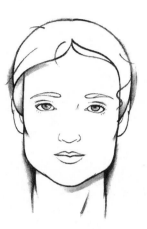

A square face tends to look as wide as it is long with easily distinguishable angles. If this is your facial shape, your best jewelry is round, oval, or soft-edged—three characteristics that will soften the squareness of your jawline. In addition, long or dangling earrings, which emphasize vertical lines, work well for a woman with a square face. Generally look for earrings that are longer than they are wide.

Simple neckwires ending in a "V" and those with a pendant attached also elongate and slim a square face. Medium to long chains, or chains with pendants attached, help the eye travel in a vertical line and make the face appear longer and narrower. Chokers and other necklaces that form a horizontal line should be avoided as they tend to emphasize width.

A pin catching a scarf or a tie in the center of a dress or blouse will also create a "V" and hence elongate and slim a square face.

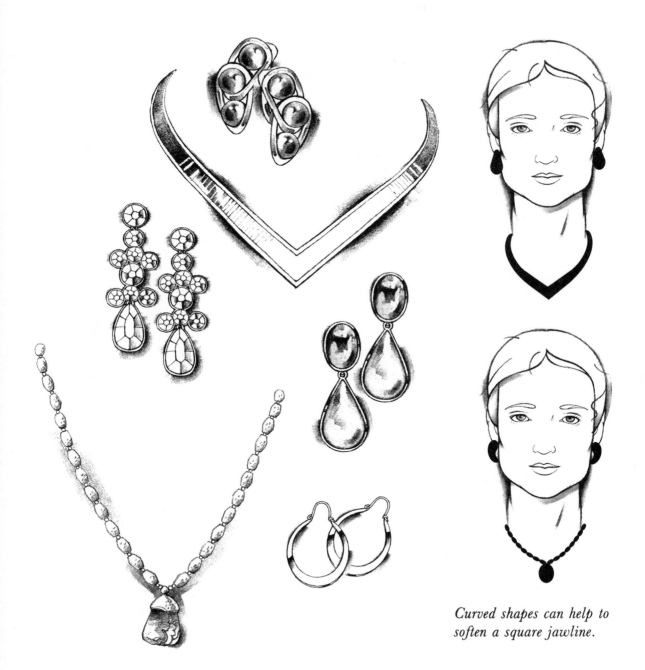

Curved shapes can help to soften a square jawline.

The rectangular face is a slight variation from the square, but it has guidelines of its own.

Sometimes this facial shape can look more like a rectangle than a square, with the same noticeable angles and equal width at the forehead and chin. However, the difference is that a rectangular-shaped face is visibly longer than a square-shaped face. If this special shape is yours, try wearing jewelry that adds width — circular earrings or those with strong horizontal lines. Don't wear drop-type dangles because these will visually lengthen your face.

The Round Face

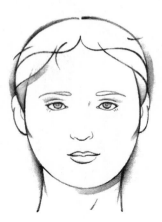

A round face is the most easily identified. In addition to being shaped like a circle, it usually has no discernible angles at the cheeks or jawline. If this is your face shape, your cheekbones and jawline are also probably softly curved.

If you want your face to appear more oval, choose earrings with vertical lines, like drops or oblongs — any shape that does not add width. Avoid circular earrings;

A goal for women with a round face is to visually add length.

For the round face, jewelry with distinct vertical lines draws the eye up and down. This has a lengthening and slimming effect.

they not only add width but also emphasize the circular shape of your face by repeating the circle at the ear. Large, round hoops have the same effect. You can add more definition to your cheekbones by choosing jewelry with angularity and sharpness in the design. Just as jewelry with curves softens the angularity of a woman with a square face, jewelry featuring strong angular designs adds definition to a round face.

A goal for this shape is to visually add length. Longer chains or strands of pearls form a strong vertical line that works well for you. Try wearing necklaces of opera length or longer, perhaps knotted at the end for more emphasis. "V" type necklaces or neckwires also work to slenderize your face. But stay away from chokers, because their horizontal line adds width to your face. When catching a scarf with a pin, center the pin rather that pinning it to one side. This will draw the eye in a vertical line, adding length and making your face seem more slender.

The Heart-shaped Face

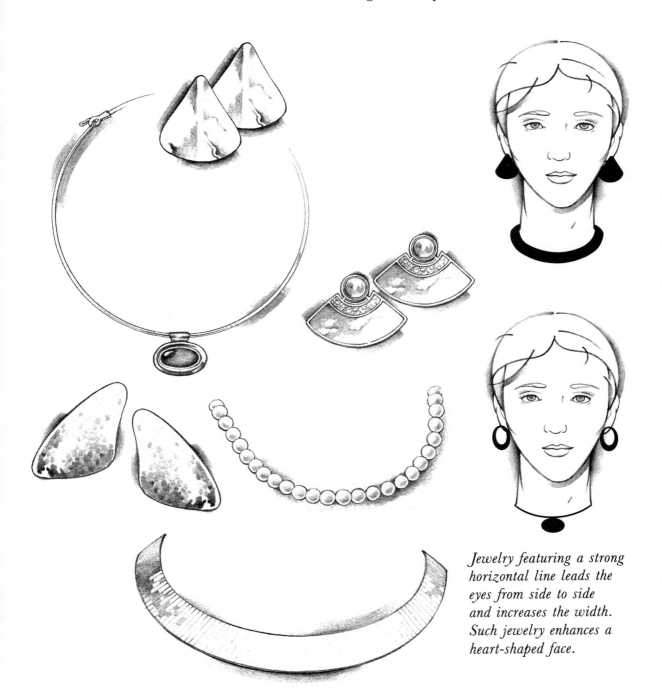

Jewelry featuring a strong
horizontal line leads the
eyes from side to side
and increases the width.
Such jewelry enhances a
heart-shaped face.

True to its descriptive name, a heart-shaped face is wide at the forehead and cheeks, then narrows to a point at the chin. If your face is this shape, you are in company with the heroines of most Victorian novels. But today you may want to soften that chin and make it seem more oval. If you do, try wearing earrings and necklaces that visually add width to the lower half of your face. Earrings that are wider at the bottom than at the top do this. For example, try some with a triangular shape, their point turned to the top. Round hoops with their curved edges can also soften the pointedness of the chin. Long, narrow earrings should be avoided because they add length and also accentuate the pointedness of the chin.

Necklaces that end in a "V" don't flatter your heart-shaped face because the "V" repeats the sharp lines of the chin. A choker or princess length works well, as their curved lines work to soften and widen the angularity of your chin.

A noticeable pin that's placed to one side or the other, or one that catches a scarf at the shoulder, will also help lead the eye in a horizontal line and tend to give your chin a wider appearance. Avoid wearing one that's pinned in the center to keep from reinforcing the pointedness of your chin.

SPECIAL CONSIDERATIONS

Necks

When selecting jewelry to adorn your face, you need to take into account your neck's shape also. Basically, necks come under four categories: they can be short or long, wide or slender. You can tell yours by looking in a mirror with your hair pulled away from your face. Look at the illustrations to help you identify the characteristics of yours.

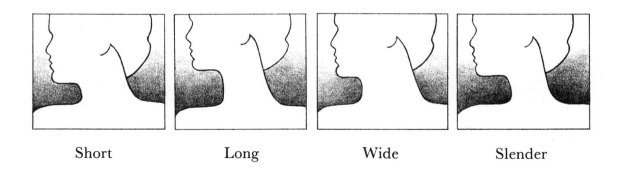

Short   Long   Wide   Slender

Choosing jewelry that works with both your neck and face is relatively easy because, most of the time, your neck's length and width is compatible with the shape of your face. Generally, the jewelry that flatters your facial shape works for your neck also.

Long or short: Does your neck look like Audrey Hepburn's? If your neck is very long like hers, you can choose necklaces featuring a strong horizontal line (choker or princess length); these help diminish the impression of length. If, however, your neck is somewhat less than swanlike and you'd like it to look longer, a long necklace that ends in a "U" or "V" and hits well below the collarbone will add length to the neck. The vertical line will lead the viewer's eye up and down and help to elongate the appearance of your neck.

Thin or wide: When you looked at your neck in the mirror, did it appear thin or wide? A full neck can be made to seem longer and slimmer by wearing a necklace with a strong vertical line (matinée length or longer). If your neck is thin, choose necklaces of short lengths (choker or princess) because they add a perception of width to your neck. In addition, you'll want to keep an eye on proportion. Big and bold necklaces can overpower a very slender neck.

Remember to keep in mind your age when choosing jewelry to wear around your neck. If excessive neck wrinkles are a problem, you can use a long necklace to pull the eye away from this area.

Other Factors

Two final factors should be considered when you select the earrings and necklaces that will be just right for you.

First is the size of your earlobes. If you have lobes that are either very large or very small, they are best minimized. Button-type or geometric-shaped clips work well for you because they cover the lobe.

The second factor is eyeglasses. If you wear glasses, usually a smaller, close-to-the-lobe earring is best for you. Large or dangling-style earrings tend to fight for attention with your glasses.

EARRINGS

Earrings in Rome, made popular by the emperor Caesar's fondness of them, were worn more often by men than women. Centuries later, Shakespeare wore one when he had his portrait made. Of course, pirates have always sported those that dangled and swept with drama. And a king of England, Charles I, favored earrings so, he went to his execution wearing a single pearl stud in his right ear.

Despite these historical precedents, today in America earrings are worn primarily by women. Your choices lie among the following types.

Earhooks   **Earhoops**   **Earposts**   **French clips**

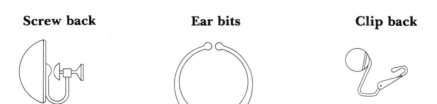

Screw back   **Ear bits**   **Clip back**

TRYING IT ON

L et's stop for a moment and backtrack. So far, you've found your facial shape and seen specifically which jewelry shapes work best for you. You've also learned some basic rules to use when choosing jewelry for your face.

Now, put all of this together with your jewelry and make an exciting discovery: there are probably many pieces in your jewelry box that bring out the best in you. Don't miss the opportunity to examine your jewelry now and try on your earrings and necklaces. Take time to determine which pieces are best for you. With a little practice and thought, the selections will become second-nature.

Viewing yourself in a full-length mirror not only aids in appreciating proportion, it also lets you see yourself and your jewelry the way other people see you.

Using these guidelines should be an experience in self-discovery, creativity, and personal growth. When you begin to try on your jewelry, don't look *just at the jewelry*. Look rather at the total effect. And be sure to view yourself in a full-length mirror. Many times when you start working with your jewelry there will be a tendency to focus only on the jewelry. This causes you to concentrate only on isolated areas of your appearance. Bear in mind that it is your total look that is the objective of selecting the right jewelry for you. All the elements of your appearance should work harmoniously and excitingly to bring out the best in you.

The design principles and how they interact with shapes are timeless and universal. Now that you are familiar with them, it's natural to apply them to your hands and wrists and the jewelry that adorns them.

CHAIN TYPES

The design of a chain affects its strength. Below, the most common chain designs are described. Generally, chain types are *full* or *flat*. Those that are flat tend to kink easier and weaken when worn with a heavy pendant. Of the full style of chains, ropes are generally the strongest.

Style	Illustration	Type
cable		full
curb		full
rope		full
herringbone		flat
serpentine		flat

3 *Jewelry for Your Hands and Wrists*

Your hands are a very effective form of communication. Without a word, they convey a lot about you—your moods, your feelings, whether you're confident or stressed, energetic or tired. Consider these familiar messages conveyed by just using your hands:

Excitement or joy: clapping or waving your hands

Anger: pounding a fist

Deep thought or concentration: drawing your fingers across your brow

Nervousness: clasping or wringing your hands

The list is almost endless. Nothing gets a point across with such ease as a simple movement of your hands. So, although they are a small part of your overall body size, hands can play a major part in your appearance. Like your face, your hands are always in view. Their unique flexibility and constant motion will quickly draw attention to them—and the jewelry you wear on them.

The jewelry on your hands is often where people "read" information and gather personal clues about you. Look at your rings for a moment. What do they tell about you? Your marital status? The number of children you have? Your educational background? Your initials?

Perhaps the month of your birth? Each of these details can be revealed by a different kind of ring.

Over the centuries, rings have come to occupy a foremost place among the five pieces of jewelry commonly worn. Today, for example,

- rings are the number-one best-selling jewelry item in America in units sold
- each year, more money is spent on rings than on any other type of jewelry
- three-fourths of all American women marrying for the first time receive an engagement ring
- almost all women wear a wedding ring at one time or another during their lifetimes

In addition to the rings you wear on your hands, one of the most functional pieces of jewelry, the watch, is commonly worn at your wrist. Because you probably refer to it many times throughout the day, it is also one of the most visible items you'll wear.

So, while it may be your face that is first noticed, your hands command equally significant attention, provide information about you, and can add to your total beauty.

Does the attention that centers on your hands and wrists work to your advantage? Does the jewelry you wear flatter, become, and enhance them? Do you have a ring that never fails to draw a compliment, yet another that never inspires a word?

CHOOSING JEWELRY TO FLATTER YOUR HANDS AND WRISTS

Choosing jewelry to complement and enhance your hands is no more difficult than choosing the jewelry that complements your face. If you've already found your facial shape and have begun selecting the earrings and necklaces that flatter it, you've been using the five principles of design. It's easy to extend that basic knowledge to the jewelry that interacts with your hands. It's simply a matter of becoming conscious of the shape of your hand, the shape of the jewelry you wear on it, and knowing how these two can work together.

Few women inherit perfectly proportioned hands any more than they inherit perfectly proportioned faces or figures. Just as with your face, the size and shape of your hands, your wrists, and your fingers directly affects the jewelry which will look best on you.

Rings and bracelets can add to your beauty. The time invested in choosing those pieces that are right for you can pay off doubly in the long run: the right jewelry not only complements your hand, but also adds to your overall appearance.

As with your face, three factors determine which jewelry shapes flatter your hands:

1) the shape of your hand
2) the shape of your jewelry
3) how these two interact.

FINDING THE PROPORTIONS OF YOUR HANDS AND WRISTS

Two factors influence the way jewelry looks on your hand: the length of your fingers and the width of your wrists.

Fingers are one of three lengths: short, average, and long.

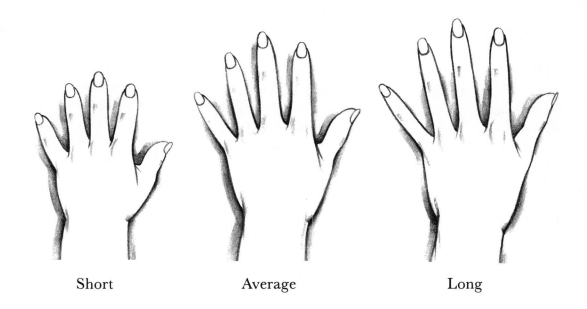

Short   Average   Long

Wrists tend to fall into two categories: broad or slender.

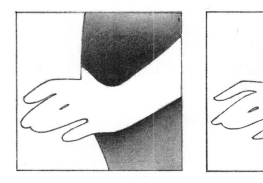

Broad   Slender

The length of your fingers has a direct effect on the ring styles or designs that enhance your hand. And, as importantly, the width of your wrist influences the bracelets or watches which work best for you. Because wrist watches are designed in bracelet form, the information about bracelets applies to watches also.

Be forewarned: determining your hand's specific type is more difficult than finding your facial shape. Because the difference between a hand with short fingers and one with long fingers may only measure a fraction of an inch, trust your eyes. In determining the type of fingers and wrists you have, your eyes and your own sense of proportion will be your best guides.

Subtle but significant differences in finger lengths and proportions make it more difficult to determine your hand shape than your face shape.

Examples of the different hands and wrists are shown here. These illustrate the proportional differences between the finger lengths and the difference between a broad and slender wrist. To determine the category into which your hands and wrists fall, first remove all your jewelry. Now look at your hands in a mirror, then compare them to these drawings. Focus on your wrists and fingers, but be sure to consider the overall impression of them in relation to your entire hand. And keep in mind that longer nails add visual length to your fingers.

Of the illustrations, which most closely resemble your fingers and your wrists? Remember, you're looking at the proportional balance. Do your fingers look long or short in relation to the rest of your hand? Does your wrist look broad or slender when you take into consideration your arms as well as your hands?

Prominent bone structure adds vertical lines to the hands and helps make them appear longer.

If you still can't tell, perhaps this suggestion will help. Look at the bone structure of your hand. An angular and prominent bone structure generally indicates hands with longer fingers and a slender wrist. The opposite type hand—a fleshy one with very little bone structure—often indicates shorter fingers and a broader wrist.

Once you have determined your finger length and wrist size, choosing jewelry to adorn them becomes much easier. You've already done this with your face—and the results are exciting. Now you can apply these same, familiar principles to your hands.

HAND TYPES

Hands with Fingers of Average Length

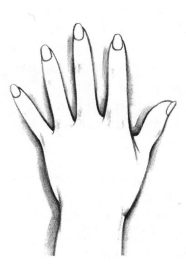

With hands, the objective is to have them appear neither too long nor too short.

This hand features fingers that are in proportion to the rest of the hand, neither excessively long nor short. This is considered to be the "ideal" for today's woman. If this is your hand, you have the same, unrestricted "wearing freedom" as women with an oval face do. Any style or shape of ring will flatter and enhance your hands. You can select your rings from simple bands to domes, from intricate gem clusters to solitaire settings.

The only guidelines you have to remember are those of proportion, one of the factors that most influences the way jewelry will look. Not long ago the only rule in choosing jewelry was "if you can afford it, wear it." This still holds true if your objective is to focus attention on your jewelry rather than yourself. However, if achieving a pleasing balance that flatters you is your

If you have hands with fingers of average length, you can wear practically any shape ring.

The length and width of a ring are important. Generally, rings that are wider than your finger or extend beyond the knuckle do not flatter.

goal, remember that people are accustomed to what they perceive as typical.

If you want your rings to be in proportion to your fingers, a good rule to remember is: do not wear rings that extend beyond your lower or upper knuckle or past the width of your finger.

Hands with Long Fingers

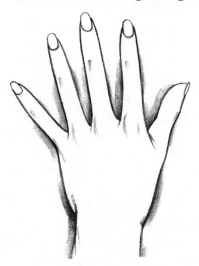

If your hand has fingers which appear long, your jewelry should give a perception of more width and less length. There are several easy ways to achieve this effect.

You can take advantage of the wide bands and the bold domes; their strong, horizontal lines make your fingers look wider and shorter. If the ring contains gemstones, two or more set in a horizontal design will also cut the visual length of your fingers. This horizontal line, especially a prominent one, will shorten and broaden the appearance of your hand.

If your fingers are long and slender and you're considering a gemstone or an engagement ring in a solitaire setting, avoid the marquise and pear-cut stones. These fancy cuts (the term "fancy" refers to all gemstone

Rings with strong horizontal lines work well on hands with long, thin fingers.

cuts other than a round shape) have a definite vertical orientation that leads the eye to the tips of your fingers, thus making them seem even longer. However, the brilliant cut, emerald cut, or a single large stone set with smaller ones on either side will work well on your hand's special shape.

One of the best things about having hands with long, slender fingers is that you can wear more than one ring on each hand. Two rings on the same hand extend the perception of a horizontal line running across your fingers and visually add width to your hand.

Hands with Short Fingers

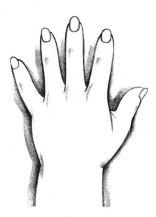

If you have short fingers, you can use your rings to make your fingers look longer and slimmer. For you, rings designed with thinner bands are best. Also, those rings with a predominantly vertical or diagonal design

will lengthen and slim down. Avoid those with strong horizontal lines, which broaden and shorten your hand.

When choosing gemstone rings, look for those with a vertical or diagonal design. For example, a number of small gemstones set diagonally across a band works well for you, because they create an illusion of length. To minimize the shortness of your fingers, avoid stones set across the band in a horizontal pattern.

Rings that feature a single gemstone or one large stone surrounded by smaller ones should also have a strong vertical line to their design. You can wear the exciting marquise and pear-shaped stones. It is best to avoid emerald-cut stones, however, because square stones emphasize a broad, rectangular look. Whatever design you choose, stay well within the knuckle.

Rings with thin bands and a dominant vertical line help make your fingers look longer and slimmer.

TYPES OF WRISTS

From earliest times, bracelets have been used to adorn various parts of the arm. Today, however, most all are worn at the wrist — as are most watches. Watches in this discussion will be treated like bracelets, because they are almost always designed in bracelet form.

Wrists have two dimensions: slender or broad. Using the illustrations as guides, which one is your wrist?

The Slender Wrist

Today, a slender wrist is considered to be the ideal. If you have a slender wrist, you can wear any type of bracelet: bangle, cuff, link, or charm. The only guidelines you have to remember are those of proportion. Check the balance of your bracelet with your height and build to see that it doesn't overpower you or become so insignificant that it has no impact.

If your wrist is very thin, look for bracelets that are smaller in diameter, because this will make your wrist seem broader in proportion. Some jewelry stores carry a choice in bangle sizes. An average-sized bangle measures 2½″ in diameter. If your wrist is very slender, look for a smaller size — one that is 2¼ inches or smaller. If your jewelry store doesn't feature small-sized bangles, try looking for them in the teen or junior sections of major department stores.

Another thing to remember if you have very thin wrists: wear a wider bracelet. The width helps give your wrist a wider look. However, keep proportion in mind when selecting your bracelet. A bracelet that is overly wide calls attention to the disproportion between the size of your wrist and the width of the bracelet.

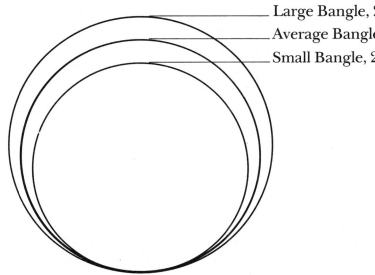

Large Bangle, 2¾″ in diameter
Average Bangle, 2½″ in diameter
Small Bangle, 2¼″ in diameter

The Broad Wrist

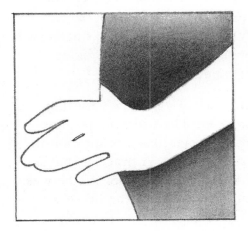

If your wrist is broad, a bracelet can help give it a more slender look. A narrow bangle, for example, works well for you. Just like the woman with a very slender wrist, you will want to look for a size bracelet (especially in bangles) that is proportional to your wrist. In some jewelry and department stores, bangles are available in graded sizes from small to large. The larger sizes, generally measuring 2¾″ or more in diameter, won't hug your wrist and work better for you. Link bracelets can also be adjusted by adding a link or two.

If you still want to wear larger, bolder bracelets, try wearing those with an open-work or latticed design. They appear to have less volume and do not broaden your wrist.

BRACELETS

Our word "bracelet" comes from the French word "bras" which actually means "arm." Originally, bracelets were functional as well as decorative. Men going into battle often wore them fitted tightly on their forearms, believing that constricting the muscles would give them extra strength.

Most bracelets today are worn by women and are usually of the following types:

Type	Definition	Illustration
Bangle	A non-flexible type bracelet that slips over the hand.	
Cuff	A non-flexible bracelet that resembles a cylindrical band. Some cuffs feature an opening in the back that slips over the wrist. Other styles have a hinged back. These slip over the wrist and fit tighter than bangles.	
Link	A type of flexible bracelet made from a series of links that have been interlocked.	
Charm	A link type of bracelet from which charms are suspended.	

Special Care Tips on Bracelets

Some bracelets, especially cuff bracelets with an open back, take a little more "TLC" than others. If you have a slip-on cuff of this type, the way it fits on your wrist is important.

When putting on a cuff bracelet, always slip it on sideways over the smallest part of your wrist. After putting it on, move your arm around and shake your hand a little. How does the cuff feel?

It may need adjusting. If it is too loose, squeeze it together gently to narrow the opening and reduce the diameter. Too tight? Enlarge it, by pulling it apart. *But do either of these things once and only once.* Repeated pulling apart and squeezing together will stress the metal, weaken it, and may ultimately cause it to break.

FINAL CONSIDERATIONS: WEARING THE RIGHT RINGS AND BRACELETS

Have you ever thought your hands and wrists were just a bit too large and wanted to know if there was something that you could do to make them seem smaller? The jewelry you wear can help.

To make your hands seem smaller, you can wear rings with a delicate styling. Those featuring flowers or motifs from nature work well for you. So do those with romantic curves, especially when the designs are rendered with a delicate, detailed craftsmanship. A simple band gives your hand a more slender appearance as long as its size is in proportion to your hand. A tiny ring appears out

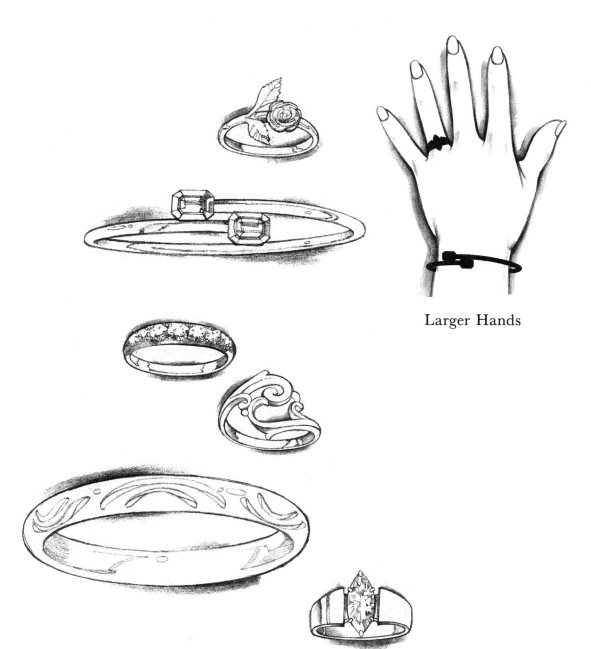

Larger Hands

Jewelry with simple bands or set with a solitaire gemstone makes your hand seem smaller and more slender.

of balance with the size of your hands and an extremely wide ring broadens the appearance of your hand.

If you want to wear a gemstone ring, choose one set with a solitaire or, at most, two stones. With a larger hand, however, you can take advantage of the exciting and unusual pear and marquise cut gemstones with their eyecatching, vertical lines leading the eye to the tips of your fingers. However, because emerald cut gemstones have a blocky, rectangular shape, they are best avoided.

As with the woman who has broad wrists, narrow bangles (especially those designed with a delicate style) make your wrist seem more slender and smaller.

No matter your hand or wrist size, the guidelines just mentioned can be used to create a sense of balance between your fingers, wrists, and hands, and between your hands and body. They allow you to choose from among those rings and bracelets that will flatter your hand and you. And as with your earrings and necklaces, you'll want to view your rings and bracelets in a full-length mirror to get the overall effect.

Now it's time to profile "personalities"— both yours and that of your jewelry!

THE HISTORY OF WEDDING RINGS

The tradition of the wedding ring dates back to the early days of Rome. The Romans had a custom of exchanging rings at the conclusion of a contract. At first this practice involved only business or commercial contracts. Gradually, it grew to include betrothal agreements as well. After the father and husband-to-be had settled on the terms of the dowry, a ring was placed on the hand of the bride-to-be. This same betrothal ring would later be used for a wedding ring at the ceremony.

The Romans are also responsible for the tradition of placing a betrothal or wedding ring on the third finger. This practice traces its origin to the belief that a nerve or vein ran from that finger to the heart.

Christians began giving and receiving wedding rings, often inscribed with symbols of their faith, around the second or third century. But it wasn't until the Middle Ages that the act of giving the ring became a part of the marriage ceremony. This ceremony offers a second explanation as to why the wedding ring is traditionally placed on the third finger of the bride. During these medieval wedding services, it was customary for the priest officiating the ceremony to touch four fingers of the bride successively (beginning with the thumb) as he said, "In the name of the Father—and of the Son—and of the Holy Ghost—Amen." As he ended with "Amen," he touched the third finger and slipped the wedding ring on that finger. And so the tradition continues today.

4 *Your Jewelry and Your Personality*

Does the jewelry you wear express what you want to say about yourself?

To answer this, take a moment to picture yourself wearing each of these pieces of jewelry on your most basic black dress. First, an enormous cubic zirconium pendant set in bold, polished silver. Next, picture yourself wearing a single strand of identically matched pearls. Third, small wooden beads. And finally, an antique cameo pin set in an elaborate but delicately filigreed silver.

Now, how would you describe the message each of these pieces communicates?

Seldom would the same word be used twice. While the enormous cubic zirconium exclaims "dramatic," "spectacular," or "flashy," the pearls pronounce "classic." The small wooden beads evoke "natural," and the cameo calls to mind "romantic." Perhaps you had different reactions, but you probably agree that each of these pieces of jewelry is a different type and each communicates its own individual and distinct message.

Jewelry — much like clothes, hair styles, or make-up — communicates a "look" or defines a "personality." As the four choices above indicate, jewelry can relate a range of messages — from quiet sophistication to soft femininity, from bold and striking to casual and easygoing. For years, clothing designers and wardrobe consultants have been insisting that styles of clothes express different statements, different looks, different personalities. Consider the different impact a Chanel suit has vs. a shirtwaist dress. Or a feathered sweater vs. a lacy blouse. A concept rapidly gaining acceptance is that specific designs or styles of jewelry also convey a look or image about the woman wearing them.

The jewelry you wear communicates a message about you, especially during first impressions.

The personality of your jewelry — the style or look of jewelry that works best for you — will be one of the four basic types: dramatic, classic, natural, or romantic. In some cases, it might be a combination of these. To determine which style is most uniquely yours, answer the following ten questions. Some questions may have several answers "right" for you, but circle only the one that you feel is the best choice.

Test

1. If you changed your looks, who would you most want to look like?

   a. Cher

   b. Jacqueline Onassis

   c. Christie Brinkley

   d. Jane Seymour

2. Which of these best describes your make-up?

   a. vivid and noticeable, emphasizing a high contrast and your lips

b. moderate, but applied in an understated look with attention to detail

c. very little and generally subtle tones

d. soft colors, usually accenting the eyes

3. Assuming all of these rings have the same dollar value, which looks the most like you?

a.

b.

c.

d.

4. You receive invitations for the following events — all scheduled for the exact same time. Which would you attend?

a. a costume party

b. the symphony

c. a picnic in the country

d. a candlelight dinner

5. Which characteristics best describe you?

    a. independent, outgoing, feeling

    b. organized, understated, cultured

    c. relaxed, down-to-earth, dependable

    d. feminine, warm, idealistic

6. At an antique jewelry sale, which piece would you be most likely to bid on?

    a. a large onyx and silver Art Deco pin

    b. a gold watch

    c. an 18-karat handmade chain

    d. a cameo necklace

7. When entertaining friends, you're most likely to have

    a. a cocktail party with all the trimmings

    b. a formal dinner using your china, silver, and crystal

    c. a backyard barbecue

    d. a candlelight dinner

8. Invited to a cocktail party, you'd feel most comfortable wearing

   a. a sequined blouse over black pants

   b. a simple black dress

   c. a print silk blouse and matching skirt

   d. a pastel-colored silk dress

9. Assuming you have just been left a great deal of money with instructions that you must spend it on jewelry, your first purchase would be

   a. a Navaho necklace, bracelet, and earrings

   b. a gold pin monogrammed with your initials and a matching gold bracelet

   c. small earstuds and a gold chain

   d. a rope of pearls and pearl drop earrings to match

10. Assuming you were trained for all the following careers, which would you choose?

    a. a star on the Broadway stage

    b. a corporate executive

    c. a tennis pro

    d. a European tour guide

Scoring

_____ A's

_____ B's

_____ C's

_____ D's

If you had more A's than any other choice, your jewelry preference tends to be dramatic in appearance. If you had more B's, you favor jewelry with a classic style and look. More C's, you prefer those pieces with a natural look. More D's, and you are partial to jewelry that offers a romantic look. If your score is divided somewhat evenly, you are very flexible and can wear a variety of looks easily.

The point of taking this quiz is to help you discover the look of jewelry that complements your personality and lifestyle. Jewelry expresses your style; it personalizes your image; it speaks to others about you.

What you have just found is your *preferred jewelry style*. More than likely it matches that of your clothes, make-up, and hair.

But does this discovery mean you have to limit your jewelry to this one image type? No more than you would limit your clothes to one. The purpose of discovering your preferred style of jewelry is to focus on the look that will help to say what you want about yourself. But there are occasions that call for a dramatic look, others that indicate a romantic look, some that suggest a natural look, and others still that dictate the classic. You may find you need some jewelry for each of the four looks.

Explore the personality of your jewelry and enjoy wearing the look that is singly yours. As you learn, don't hesitate to experiment with other looks as the occasion or mood demands. This is the fun part of wearing jewelry. In experimenting with and using looks other than your preferred jewelry look, you can fully express yourself with jewelry.

THE DRAMATIC LOOK IN JEWELRY

If you prefer jewelry that's bold and daring, jewelry that grabs attention, provokes comments, and catches the eye, then dramatic jewelry is for you. These are the big and bold pieces characterized by tremendous impact.

Often, dramatic jewelry suggests a sense of the unconventional. The style, design, and materials of dramatic pieces rank among the trend-setters and rule-breakers in jewelry. Dramatic examples are the 3″ sterling silver Christmas ornaments that have been converted to earrings. Dramatic pieces are also large hammered bracelets that curl around your wrists. Many dramatic pieces are designed to have a short life span and are therefore usually made from less precious materials. An exception is the large gemstone which, while dramatic, will also be kept for generations.

Dramatic pieces are often made by experimental processes and materials. For this reason they may be one-of-a-kind creations. When they include gemstones in their design, the stones are usually distinguished by an uncommon size or cut. Gemstone cuts can be free-form or one of those cuts described as "fancy." (See the chart of common gemstone cuts, Chapter Seven.) Extremes, angularity, and boldness characterize dramatic jewelry. Many times, dramatic pieces use a high polish to attract attention. However, they can also be rough-looking with primitive designs. Antique pieces having a dramatic look include many of those designed during the Art Deco period of the 1920s and 1930s.

Wearing Dramatic Jewelry: What It Can Do For You

Unique and attention-getting, dramatic pieces call forth emotion and spotlight attention on your flair for drama. This type jewelry may complement an innovative personality, one that's uninhibited and has a striking theatrical quality. It's important to note, however, that because of its size and dramatic flair, dramatic jewelry calls attention to the jewelry first and then to the wearer.

Dramatic jewelry also gives an impression of the wearer's self-confidence. Yet, because of its use of the distinctive, the innovative, or the unusual, it also offers an approachable quality. Dramatic pieces of jewelry often function as ice-breakers, inviting conversations about some aspect of their design.

THE CLASSIC LOOK IN JEWELRY

Classic jewelry avoids trendiness in style in favor of lasting, traditional designs. Often pieces of classic jewelry fall into predictable designs that are reinterpreted year after year because they are flattering to so many women and are wearable and appropriate

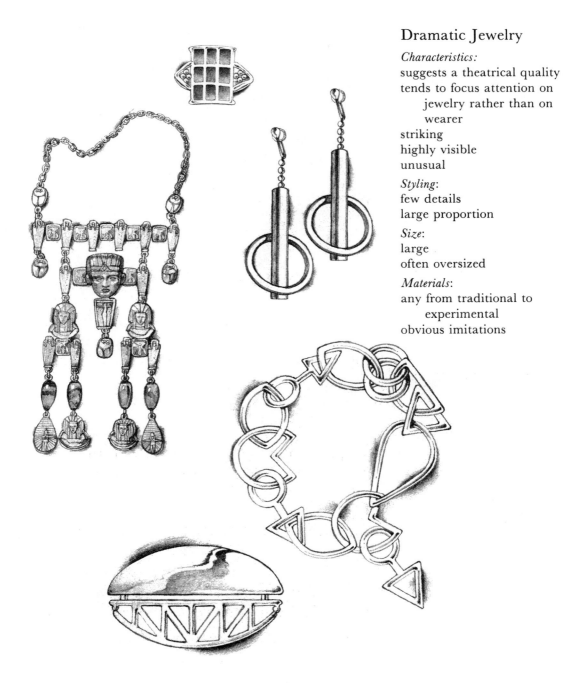

Dramatic Jewelry

Characteristics:
suggests a theatrical quality
tends to focus attention on
    jewelry rather than on
    wearer
striking
highly visible
unusual

Styling:
few details
large proportion

Size:
large
often oversized

Materials:
any from traditional to
    experimental
obvious imitations

on many occasions. Symmetry and harmony in design and color characterize classic jewelry. Classic jewelry is never severe.

In fact, classic jewelry avoids all extremes — of fashion, of size, of design, and of emotional impact — in favor of an expected design which usually features some simple geometric shape (for example, a circle, triangle, square, or rectangle). Classic jewelry is distinguished by the absence of anything that hangs, swings, or dangles. What does set classic pieces apart is a fine quality of design and workmanship which is obvious and appreciable.

Gemstone cuts in classic jewelry avoid the unusual and the striking in favor of the more traditional cuts like the brilliant or the emerald cut. In pearls, a classic neck piece would be a medium-length strand of uniformly matched pearls.

Wearing Classic Jewelry: What It Can Do For You

Because of its traditional styling, its simple, uncluttered lines, and its high quality of workmanship, classic jewelry conveys a feeling of feminine dignity. It sends a message of competence and control, and an air of refined elegance. One of classic jewelry's best traits is that it combines unobtrusively with your clothes, thereby allowing you to be the star. Unlike dramatic jewelry, classic jewelry contributes effectively to you, not to itself. That's one reason why it is often appropriate in business or professional situations.

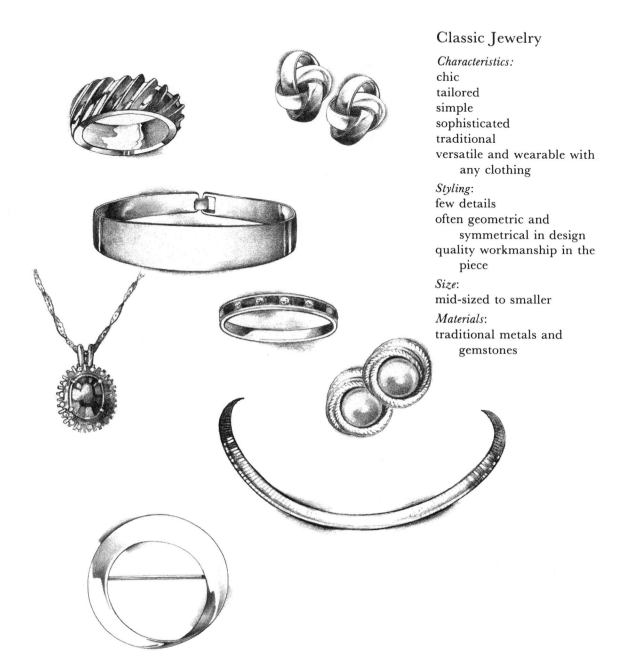

Classic Jewelry

Characteristics:
chic
tailored
simple
sophisticated
traditional
versatile and wearable with
    any clothing

Styling:
few details
often geometric and
    symmetrical in design
quality workmanship in the
    piece

Size:
mid-sized to smaller

Materials:
traditional metals and
    gemstones

THE NATURAL LOOK IN JEWELRY

Natural jewelry provides a down-to-earth, quiet, and unassuming look. Often natural jewelry designs retain some of the simplicity of styling of the classic look, but in a smaller size and a more relaxed way. At other times, however, natural jewelry takes its designs from the warmth and charm of nature. Thus, basic chains and simple bracelets as well as a pendant with an easily recognizable animal or flower motif, or even a pin in the design of something as familiar as a sea shell, all fit into the category of natural jewelry. Other examples of jewelry with a natural look are carved wooden beads and ethnic jewelry (as long as the size remains small). Regardless of the motif, natural jewelry is characterized by three qualities: it is easy to wear, comfortable, and generally lightweight.

Wearing Natural Jewelry: What It Can Do For You

Natural jewelry relates a feeling of informality, of a relaxed, easygoing manner. It expresses friendliness, warmth, and familiarity. Natural jewelry doesn't seem artificial nor does it seem sophisticated.

Although natural jewelry won't demand or command attention as dramatic jewelry does, its familiar motif can initiate conversations or draw comments. The simplicity and small size of natural designs serve to quietly complement each other as well as virtually every outfit with which they are worn.

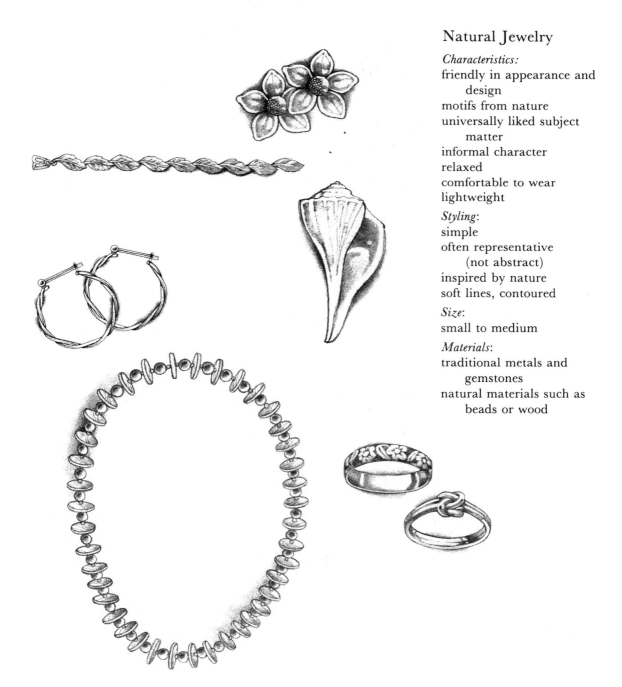

Natural Jewelry

Characteristics:
friendly in appearance and
    design
motifs from nature
universally liked subject
    matter
informal character
relaxed
comfortable to wear
lightweight

Styling:
simple
often representative
    (not abstract)
inspired by nature
soft lines, contoured

Size:
small to medium

Materials:
traditional metals and
    gemstones
natural materials such as
    beads or wood

THE ROMANTIC LOOK IN JEWELRY

O ther than the dramatic, romantic jewelry is the easiest type to recognize. Delicate in detail, but eloquent in effect, romantic jewelry includes all those motifs that have come to represent love and romance over the years — hearts, bows, lace, roses, etc. In addition to these, pieces characterized by delicate details, gentle curves, or open-work designs also give a romantic look. So do ornately filigreed, open-work designs of lacy, woven patterns.

Although romantic jewelry can be finished in many ways, a soft matte finish usually suggests a hint of the romantic look. All in all, romantic pieces are those that look as if they came from your grandmother's jewelry box, or if new, could at least fit in there comfortably.

Gemstones with detailed characteristics and gentle curves also distinguish a romantic look. Cuts like the heart, marquise, and pear, and swirls of channel-set baguettes offer a romantic look, as do pastel (especially pink and purple) gemstones. But, of course, the setting must also be one of romantic design.

While a classic woman wears a simple, mid-length strand of pearls, the romantic woman loops or twists a longer strand or uses several strands of smaller pearls as a choker. Mother-of-pearl jewelry is also a staple of the romantic jewelry wardrobe.

Many pieces of antique jewelry offer a romantic look, especially those dating from the Edwardian, Victorian, or Art Nouveau periods. Even recently made pieces that borrow a motif from times past, like a carousel horse, characterize a romantic style.

Romantic Jewelry

Characteristics:
romantic or nostalgic
    images
soft, graceful lines
delicate
full curves
evokes thoughts of times
    past
traditional romantic motifs
    (hearts, bows, lace,
    roses)
a theatrical quality
feminine

Styling:
rich details
intricate, delicate
open or pierced
ornate
feminine
many larger designs feature
    open-work style to
    maintain a delicate
    appearance

Size:
medium to large

Materials:
traditional
soft-colored gemstones

Wearing Romantic Jewelry: What It Can Do For You

If you want to convey a subtle feminine look which is soft and delicate, then romantic jewelry can help. This look in jewelry complements clothes with the same characteristics — gentle curves, soft lines, delicate details. The style is great for late night dinners or romantic rendezvous. You can also use it to provide a hint of femininity to a classic suit, making a subtle but appropriate statement in the work place.

The relatively large size and familiar motif of most romantic jewelry does attract attention. As with dramatic jewelry, the design of the jewelry is more important than the materials because of the emotional connotation.

The key words describing the look romantic jewelry evokes are soft, gentle, and feminine.

ACHIEVING SEVERAL LOOKS

But what if. . .

. . . you've always worn classic jewelry and clothes and you've been invited to attend a cast party after a Broadway opening?

. . . you're most comfortable in natural jewelry and clothes, but you've been invited to dinner by a man in whom you have a romantic interest?

. . . you love dramatic jewelry and clothes, but you have a job interview — with a bank?

What if . . . what if . . . what if?

Although you've just found the type of jewelry that you are most comfortable in, there are going to be those days when you want to break out of the usual routine. It could be for a special occasion or it could just be a time when you want to show a different side of yourself.

This is a time you'll want to use your jewelry to cross over to another look. Each of the four jewelry styles makes a different statement and evokes a different response from the viewer. As the basic black dress with the four different pieces at the first of this chapter pointed out, a change of jewelry can be one of the easiest ways to convey a different side of you or provide an appropriate look for a special occasion.

Each of the four jewelry styles makes a different statement and evokes a different response.

When you begin going through your jewelry collection, you may find you have no dramatic or romantic jewelry. Or, perhaps in your entire collection there is just a single piece of classic or natural jewelry. Take just a moment to consider these gaps. How much do you need the look you're missing? Do you have occasions in your lifestyle that call for the wearing of this look? Have you ever wanted to try the image, but didn't know how?

A trip to the house of a good friend who has and wears jewelry looks that are different from yours can be a revealing experience. In trying on hers (keeping in mind to select the shapes that flatter you) you can express yourself with different styles of jewelry. Why not take your jewelry along to let her express another side of her personality?

You'll get the most out of your jewelry when you can comfortably wear all the jewelry looks as your mood or the occasion demands.

5 *You, Color, and Your Jewelry*

U nless you belong to that rare percentage of the population who sees the world in tones of black and white, color plays a significant role in your life. Color affects how you feel: certain colors excite you, others calm you. Color evokes certain responses: some colors attract you, others annoy you. And, equally as important, some colors bring out the best in you while others do little for — or even detract from — your natural beauty.

Recently, many best-selling books about color have attracted a great deal of attention. Contending that color may be the key to beauty, image, and even power, these books and their principles have become widely acclaimed, accepted, and applied. With all its exciting possibilities (and even a few pitfalls), color now occupies a prominent place on the personal beauty scene.

However, most of this information about color has been applied to the wearing of clothing and make-up. But what about color in jewelry? For instance, a blue sapphire vs. a green emerald? Or a golden glow vs. a silvery shimmer? Jewelry has incorporated color from ancient times — from coral to shells; from feathers to gemstones. Because jewelry is often worn next to your skin and near your hair and eyes, its color interacts with that of your complexion. Wearing the right color jewelry is an important ingredient in enhancing your beauty.

If the color is wrong, the jewelry will look wrong and the effect you've worked to create is lost.

Now comes the fun of applying all this exciting new information about color to the jewelry and gemstone colors you wear. It's easy. The same principles that guide the use of color in your clothes and make-up also apply to your selection of jewelry.

WHAT IS COLOR?

To understand what color can and can't do for you, it helps to first consider what color is.

In its most simple definition, color is actually a series of light waves sent back (reflected) from anything. Some waves are short, some are long. Waves from a purple amethyst, for example, are very short; those from a ruby are almost twice as long. Your eye just "reads" the length of the waves and "tells" you the color.

Of the infinite number of colors that greet your eyes each day, there are only three pure colors used to create the various pigments: red, blue, and yellow. These are called primary because from these three colors all others can be created. For example, mixing any two of the primary colors gives the three secondary colors: green, violet, and orange.

Look at the simple color wheel, which depicts the primary and secondary colors and further variations of them. The color wheel is important in determining the most flattering colors in the jewelry you wear. You may have already noticed that the left side of the wheel has been marked "warm" while the right side is designated as "cool." "Warm" colors have a yellow undertone or base. "Cool" colors have a blue undertone or base.

Keeping the colors of nature in mind can help you understand the cool—warm concept of colors. For example, the "warmth" of a red sunset or the "coolness" of a green shade tree.

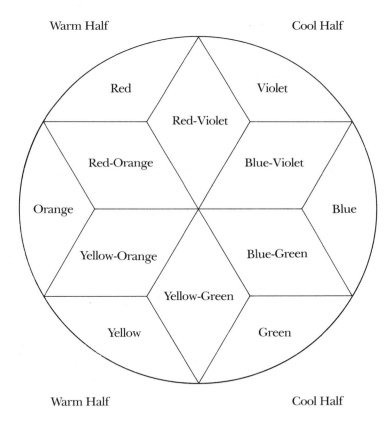

Warm Half   Cool Half

Red   Violet

Red-Violet

Red-Orange   Blue-Violet

Orange   Blue

Yellow-Orange   Blue-Green

Yellow-Green

Yellow   Green

Warm Half   Cool Half

COLORS AND YOU

How does this warm-cool factor affect you? All skin color has either a cool (blue) undertone or a warm (yellow) undertone to it. Your skin tone is the most important factor to consider when finding the color of jewelry that will work to complement your unique beauty.

All you need to do to wear colors excitingly well is to team up warm or cool colors — of clothes, of make-up, and of *jewelry* — with the same complexion tone. If you have already had your colors analyzed by a professional color consultant, then you're probably familiar with this concept and have been selecting your jewelry accordingly. If you haven't, the first step in using the color of the jewelry you wear to your best advantage is to find which color undertone your skin has.

The Skin Tone Test

Some women's skin tone is obvious. The undertone (blue or yellow) is readily seen with just a glance in the mirror. But if you're not quite sure about yours, check the area of skin on your forearm between your wrist and elbow, or some other untanned area of your body. You're looking for the *undertone*, the blue or golden cast to your skin. This determines whether your coloring is cool or warm. To help you see it more readily, slip something white like a towel under your arm to neutralize the influence of any nearby colors. Be sure to do this in a natural light. Artificial light can often produce an unnatural cast.

Still having trouble?

It may help to look for your skin tone with a friend or friends. Often they are more objective. Also, it is often easier to see your own coloring when you can compare and contrast it to someone else's.

Does your skin have a warm or cool undertone — golden or blue? This is the "base" of your coloring.

Determining Your Color Category

Using this information you can now determine your own personal color type. Keeping in mind the warm or cool undertone of your skin, use the Seasonal Color Chart to locate the color of your hair, eyes, and skin. The categories on this chart are arranged according to the seasonal color system. This system, introduced by Johannes Itten in the 1920s, divides women's coloring into four groups: spring, summer, winter, or autumn. The seasonal names were chosen because the colors of each group fit adjectives which describe that season.

The names spring, summer, autumn, and winter were chosen because the colors of each group are common to and evoke feelings of that particular season.

Because many women have had their colors analyzed according to this seasonal system, it will be used as the principal reference for selecting jewelry colors that complement your special complexion. If you had your "colors done" according to another system, you may want to refer to the chart on the following page which cross-references many of the color systems.

Understanding your color palette — its possibilities as well as its limitations — will assist you in selecting the jewelry colors that flatter your complexion.

SEASONAL COLORS

	Cool Seasons		**Warm Seasons**	
	Winter	Summer	Autumn	Spring
Skin	very white	white with pale	ivory	ivory
	rosy beige	pink cheeks	golden beige	peach
	olive	light olive	deep golden	golden beige
	brown	pink beige		
	black	neutral beige		
Hair	black	platinum blonde	auburn	blonde:
	dark brown	light brown	red	strawberry
	salt and	dark blonde (ash)	red highlights	flaxen
	pepper	pearl gray		golden
	white			dark with
				golden
				highlights
Eyes	dark brown	blue	dark brown	clear blue
	hazel	green	olive	bright green
	deep blue	hazel	green	amber
			blue	

A Cross Reference of Color Systems

Winter	Summer	Autumn	Spring
Contrast	Gentle	Muted	Light Bright
Sunrise	Sunlight	Sunset	Sunlight

Whether it's the color of an elaborate gemstone or that of simple, hand-painted wooden beads, the color of your jewelry has the ability to enhance or detract from your overall beauty.

Please note: The following section considers many details about jewelry and colors, and some of the most common materials used in jewelry have been included. Many of these will be familiar, others may not. Information about the materials that go into making jewelry (gemstones, metals, plastics, wood, etc.) has been included in the section entitled "Buying the Right Jewelry." If you are unfamiliar with a gemstone or other material listed here, you can turn to that section to find out about it.

WINTER (Contrast, Sunrise)

Long-stemmed red roses. Fields blanketed in white snow. The blackest of nights. These are the color schemes suitable for women with a winter coloring.

Over half the women in America are winters. In general, they have intense coloring with dark hair and eyes. (An exception is the platinum blonde with blue eyes.) Women with olive skin, as well as virtually all Oriental and black women, fall into the winter category. Whatever their hair and eye coloring, all winters are guided in their color selections by the cool, blue undertone of their skin.

Winters thrive on cool, vivid colors and high contrast in their jewelry: a necklace of shiny black and white beads, earrings of onyx and silver, deep cornflower blue sapphires, blue-black pearls. The rich colors or bold contrast of this type of jewelry serves to offset their strong coloring.

Because of the cool, blue undertone of their complexion, women that are winters are complemented by a metal that is white or silver-toned. The precious metals platinum, white gold, and silver and non-precious metals like chrome, aluminum, or stainless steel work best for you if you have a winter's coloring.

If you are a winter and love the look of yellow gold, mixing the metals in your jewelry may be the answer. The popular silver-gold mixes can give you the elegance of gold but the color benefit of silver. Just remember to keep the silver tone next to your skin. Earrings, rings, and bracelets with a border of silver-colored metal and a center of gold-colored metal do this. Or use gold in your pins which are worn on clothing and are farther away from your skin, hair, and eyes.

If winter is your color category, your gemstone choices are wide and varied. Remember to look for the cool blue cast to the stone. For example, rubies look wonderful on you when they are the optimum color of rubies — a red with just a hint of blue in the color. However, you may find some rubies on the market with a yellow undertone. Just let the "suggested list" shown here serve as a guideline, not an absolute. You'll have to examine each gemstone (or any other colored piece of jewelry) individually and evaluate that gemstone's unique color and its appropriateness for you.

A Winter and Her Jewelry:

Colors of jewelry:

black
white
gray
navy
red
deep hot pink

Colors to avoid in jewelry:

orange
gold
rust
peach
beige/brown
olive
pastels

Metals:

platinum
silver
white gold
stainless steel
chrome
nickel
white metal
aluminum

Gemstones:

garnets
amethysts
coral
diamond
ruby
sapphire (blue)
spinel (red)
tanzanite
blue tourmaline
lapis lazuli (deep blue)
jet
black onyx

Pearls:

white
gray
black

SUMMER (Gentle, Sunlight)

H eather across the hillsides. Pink orchids. A pastel
   landscape. These are the backdrops that become
a woman with summer coloring.

Like winter, summer is also a blue-based (cool)
season. But there the similarity ends. Summers are
recognized by their gentle coloring, a subtle blending
of soft shades rather than the bold contrast of winters.
In fact, most often summers are blondes — or were so
when they were children. This, combined with their
lighter skin color and eyes which are most often blue
or green, gives summers the look of softness.

If winters look well in contrast, summers simply shine
when wearing the gentlest of cool pastels in their jewelry:
a necklace of carved jade, earrings of filigreed silver,
light purple amethysts, pearls with a rosy hue. The soft
pastel tones of the jewelry blend with, rather than
overpower, a summer's soft coloring.

A cool white or silver-toned metal best complements
the blue undertone of a summer's complexion. In
precious metals, this can be silver, platinum, or white
gold. In non-precious it may range from stainless steel
to pewter. If you are a summer and want to wear gold,
try rose-toned gold. However, if yellow gold is a "must"
for you, try wearing it in combination with a silver-toned
metal. As with winters, be sure to place the silver metal
next to your skin. You can also wear gold in pins placed
on clothing away from the skin.

Gemstone preferences for a summer follow the rules
of "soft and cool" also. Look for a cool cast and a lighter

color in the gemstones you wear. For example, dark purple amethysts work well for a winter, but a lighter shade flatters a summer. Pink gemstones are among the best choices for you if you have a summer coloring.

A Summer and Her Jewelry:

Colors of jewelry:

blue
rose
purple
navy
aqua
blue-reds

Colors to avoid in jewelry:

black
white
gold
orange
yellow
yellow-beige

Metals:

platinum
silver
white gold
stainless steel
pewter
rose-toned metals
rose-colored gold

Gemstones:

amethyst (light)
coral (pink)
diamond
kunzite
sapphires (pink and
    light blue)
pink spinel
pink tourmaline
blue tourmaline
green tourmaline
rhodolite garnet (light
    pink/purple)
tanzanite (light)

Pearls:

white with a rose cast
rose
light gray

AUTUMN (Muted, Sunset)

A fiery sunset. Maple leaves after the first frost. A dense forest of green. These are the colors that frame an autumn's special coloring.

While autumns are the rarest season, the range of colors that complement them are by no means narrow. The whole palette of earth and autumn colors is at their beck and call. Autumns are characterized by a warm, golden undertone to their skin and are often redheads or have red highlights in their hair. Most often they have green or brown eyes.

The warm undertone to their skin is the foundation of their jewelry color selections. Rich, warm selections such as a necklace of natural wooden beads, earrings of brass and copper, deep green emeralds, an amber pendant, a creamy strand of pearls can enhance an autumn's coloring. These pure earth tones balance and complement the warm, intense colors of an autumn's complexion.

The warm, golden undertone of an autumn's skin harmonizes with gold-toned metals. This opens up exciting choices such as copper, brass, and bronze, as well as yellow gold or gold-toned pieces. Pieces made from tortoise shell and jewelry crafted from wood also work well for an autumn.

An autumn's gemstone choices resemble a fall landscape in colors — emeralds, amber, garnets, golden sapphires, green tourmalines. If you are an autumn, remember to keep in mind that your best gemstones are those with a yellow undertone to them. You may find emeralds on the market that vary from a green with yellow to pure green to green with blue undertone. If you are unsure, hold several unset stones of varying hues next to your skin. This should make the difference apparent.

An Autumn and Her Jewelry:

Colors of jewelry:

brown
beige
orange
mustard
orange-red
green
teal
gold

Colors to avoid
in jewelry:

black
pink
navy
blue-red
gray
fuchsia

Metals:

yellow gold
brass
copper
bronze

Gemstones:

tsavorite garnets
amber
diamond
green tourmaline
    (deep)
chrome tourmaline
    (deep)
citrine (deep)
emerald
peridot
sapphire (golden)
golden topaz

Pearls:

cream
gold
off-white

SPRING (Light Bright, Sunlight)

Fields of wildflowers. A single daffodil. The blue-green of the sea. A basket of just-ripened peaches. A spring reflects these gentle colors.

Springs usually have blonde hair — strawberry, flaxen, golden, or even golden brown. Most often their eyes are blue, although they can be green or amber. Springs can have freckles. But the one thing all springs have in common is a warm, yellow (golden) undertone to their skin.

Springs flourish on warm, clear colors in their jewelry: amber beads, gold earrings, aquamarines and blue topaz, a strand of light, creamy pearls. The warm, fresh colors don't overpower their delicate coloring.

With their warm undertone, springs fare well in metals with a gold tone. If you are a spring, be aware that copper, bronze, and brass are often too strong for you. Jewelry of mixed metals works well if you remember to keep a golden tone closest to your skin.

If spring is your color, look for the warmer, lighter color of a stone. For example, look for a lighter green peridot, a lighter turquoise, light green emeralds, yellow (rather than deep golden) sapphires. Again, be sure to look at the stone in a natural (but not bright) light; hold it against your skin. It is also a good idea to compare several stones to see which works best for you.

A Spring and Her Jewelry:

Colors of jewelry:

brown
camel
aqua
peach
yellow
clear red

Colors to avoid in jewelry:

fuchsia
burgundy
black
white
dark gray
blue red

Metals:

yellow gold
gold-toned metals

Gemstones:

aquamarine
coral (peach-colored)
citrine
diamond
emerald
peridot
yellow sapphire
blue topaz
green tourmaline
turquoise
tsavorite garnet
padparadscha (pinkish-
    orange sapphire)
golden topaz
zircon

Pearls:

cream
cream with a peach
    overtone

A Final Note

As you try different colors of jewelry, consider the shape and the color carefully. A full-length mirror will help you get the total effect. And if you are still having trouble determining your exact color category, for example, between a spring and a summer, one final — and usually decisive — test is to compare silver and gold tones next to your complexion.

Which looks best? If you still can't tell, wear one of each. Still not sure? Ask a few friends.

Jewelry which combines both gold and silver flatters most women — just make sure the appropriate color is worn next to your skin.

Some women have spent years collecting one color of jewelry — silver-toned or gold-toned — when they discover they really look better in the other. If this has happened to you, combining the two metal colors may be the answer. Remember to keep the color that best complements your complexion closest to your skin. This means if you have a gold cuff and have found you wear silver better, surround it by two silver bangles. Or if you wear gold better, do just the opposite.

Discovering your best colors goes a long way in finding the right jewelry for you. And it should also simplify your shopping. Now that you know what shapes, colors, and styles to look for in jewelry, the remainder of the book is dedicated to helping you make your jewelry purchases with confidence and enjoyment.

Winter Color Palette

Summer Color Palette

Autumn Color Palette

Spring Color Palette

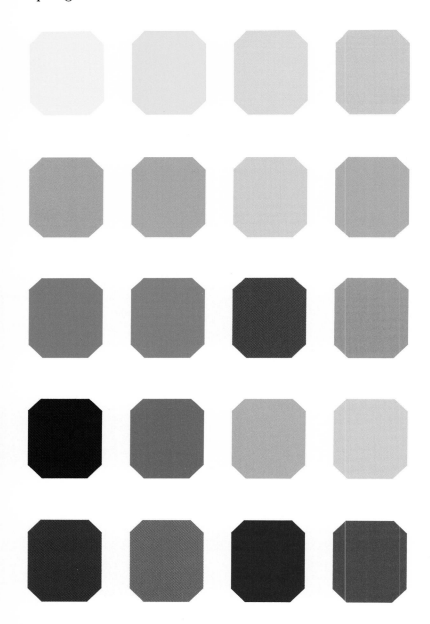

COLOR PROFILES

Color	Root Derived From	Associations/ Connotations	Common Phrases Using the Color
Green	from Old English *grene*	the earth	"green with envy" "greenhorn"
Blue	from Middle English *bleu*	baby boys sky truth constancy	"blue Monday" "blueblood" "blue funk" "blue ribbon" "bolt from the blue"
Purple	from *purpuran,* meaning a color reserved for the use of an imperial ruler	power royalty spirituality nostalgia	"purple with rage"
Red	from Sanscrit *rudhira* meaning "blood"	blood fire patriotism anger danger	"see red" "paint the town red" "red carpet treatment" "red flag" "red herring" "red letter day"
Pink	*rose* means pink in Romance languages	baby girls	"in the pink" "tickled pink" "everything coming up roses"
Orange	from the fruit	fire flames malevolence	
Yellow	Indo-European word *ghelwo* means "related to gold"	cheerfulness treachery cowardice ripening grain	"yellow-bellied" "yellow journalism"

Part
II

Buying
the Right Jewelry

6 *The Jewelry Types: Costume, Bridge, and Fine*

You've learned how to wear jewelry to your advantage: how to select the earrings and necklaces that bring out the best in your face, the rings and bracelets that flatter your hand's shape, the jewelry look that expresses your personality and fits with your lifestyle, and the colors of metals and gemstones that work best for your special complexion.

However, in trying to put this all together using the jewelry you own, have you discovered some gaps in your collection? Are there some additions you'd like to make?

It's time to think about buying jewelry. But approaching any jewelry counter without a solid understanding of the materials that make up that jewelry is like running a marathon without training for it—it's exhausting and you're seldom a winner.

It doesn't have to be that way.

Buying jewelry can be positive and exciting. And often you may find bargains. You can make wise, lasting investments and choose just the right piece to creatively stretch this season's wardrobe. You can find those pieces you will wear often—jewelry that is so "right" it gives a lifetime of wearing pleasure.

But as with a marathon, to be a "winner" when it

comes to buying jewelry, you have to train for it. "Training" in this instance means learning about the materials that go into making jewelry. Simply put, it's knowing what to *look* for as well as what to *look out* for in jewelry. The materials that make up each piece will be key factors in its quality, value, price, and life span.

TYPES OF JEWELRY

If, while reading the first section of this book, you looked through your jewelry collection to find those pieces that work best for you, you probably came across a wide range of jewelry types. Some costly, some inexpensive. Pieces made from glass, pieces made from gemstones. Antique pieces as well as new acquisitions. All these pieces of jewelry fall into one of three categories: costume jewelry, bridge jewelry, or fine jewelry.

Becoming familiar with each of these categories— their characteristics, cost, and content—is the first step in learning to buy the right jewelry. Each type has a distinct place in today's world of fashion, and each may have a significant role in your jewelry wardrobe. Often a well-balanced, versatile, and working jewelry collection will contain some of all three types. And, of course, mixing the three styles is not only acceptable, it can provide an exciting look of freshness and individuality. When considering the roles and the importance of each type of jewelry to you, four criteria can be used:

(1) Does it fit into your lifestyle?
(2) Does it meet the needs of your work and social life?
(3) Does it fit your budget?
(4) How long do you want to keep it?

Costume Jewelry

If all the types of jewelry occupied a straight line, costume jewelry would be at one end and fine jewelry at the other. They are opposites in the world of jewelry. Where fine jewelry is usually expensive, costume jewelry is relatively inexpensive. Fine jewelry is classic in style, while costume jewelry is usually trendy. Fine jewelry is designed to last, to be handed down from generation to generation. Costume jewelry is created to be "just right" for the moment. With this great diversity, you can see why you might use some of both types in your collection.

Costume jewelry is a relative newcomer to the world of jewelry — less than a century old. It was a result of the changing times marking the end of the Victorian era and World War I. With the 1920s came a resurgence of fashion in clothing. The old, classic, expensive fine jewelry couldn't keep pace with the fashion. So the glitzy, trendy, inexpensive alternative of costume jewelry was born. Supported and glamorized by famous personalities like Coco Chanel, it gained immediate acceptance.

Today's costume jewelry ranges from plastic pieces costing less than a dollar to intricate creations costing thousands of dollars. In general, costume jewelry can be divided into three types:

- replicas of classic gold jewelry designs
- plastic pieces created in fashionable of colors
- showy pieces with unusual metals and imitation gems

Costume jewelry is still strongly linked with the fashion industry. In fact, it is most often sold in specialty fashion dress stores or department stores rather than fine jewelry stores.

Costume jewelry is sometimes referred to as fashion jewelry because of its trendy styles and close ties to the fashion industry.

Costume jewelry offers many unique advantages. First among them is affordability. Although designer pieces can run to several hundreds or several thousands of dollars, most pieces fall into an affordable range. This affordability allows you to experiment with costume jewelry. Mistakes made in buying costume jewelry are not nearly so costly as those in bridge or fine jewelry. Another advantage costume jewelry brings with it is fashion forward designs. No matter what the clothing industry's changes are, costume jewelry is quick to meet them.

Bridge Jewelry

Bridge jewelry, like costume jewelry, is the product of changing times. The key to its popular acceptance rests with women reentering the workforce in record numbers over the past couple of decades. These women viewed jewelry differently from the preceding generation: they wanted jewelry that was fashionable, that had intrinsic value, but that didn't demand a major investment. Their need for "fashion with enduring quality" brought bridge jewelry into being.

Characteristics that distinguish bridge jewelry are the use of materials with intrinsic value in combination with fashionable, but lasting designs.

Bridge jewelry spans the gap between the trendy designs and affordability of costume jewelry and the classic designs and expensive cost of fine jewelry. This "middle" position allows it to take many forms and be made from a variety of materials.

Three common threads link all pieces of bridge jewelry: first, the use of precious metals (gold filled, gold plated, some karat gold, and sterling silver); second, a relatively inexpensive price; and third, fashionable designs. Like costume jewelry, bridge jewelry is available in clothing boutiques and special sections of department stores. But, like fine jewelry, it is also sometimes found in jewelry stores.

Fine Jewelry

Fine jewelry — famous examples of it are Princess Diana's sapphire and diamond ring, Elizabeth Taylor's enormous natural pearl (the Perlingua), the Hope Diamond, the British Crown jewels.

Most likely you have pieces of fine jewelry too, like your diamond engagement ring, an antique gold bangle, a string of cultured pearls, or a family heirloom brooch.

Fine jewelry pieces are crafted using gold or platinum. When a piece of fine jewelry is set with gemstones, they are usually precious and costly. To purchase a piece of fine jewelry represents a substantial monetary investment. As a result, most women buy it for a lifetime of wear, and usually as something that can be passed on to future generations. For this reason, most styles of fine jewelry are simple, classic, and timeless, created using the best in quality and craftsmanship.

EVALUATING YOUR PURCHASES

Becoming an informed consumer when it comes to buying jewelry means learning about the materials that go into making jewelry. It is not as complicated as it sounds, for you don't have to be as well informed as a jewelry manufacturer. Only expensive purchases need be appraised extensively by you. You can live with a $10 mistake. But as zeros are added to the price of the piece, mistakes become more critical.

The more expensive a piece of jewelry is, the more important it is to know exactly what you are buying.

Gemstones and precious metals are the two areas in which jewelry-buying mistakes can be made most easily. And not coincidentally, they are the two most costly aspects of jewelry. That's why each is detailed in succeeding chapters.

Once you learn what goes into jewelry, you know what to look for when you shop. Then you can buy without intimidation and make those purchases with confidence and assurance.

THE TYPES OF JEWELRY

Type	Advantages	Gemstones	Metals	Cost	Where to buy?
Costume	affordable trendy	artificial	non-precious	affordable	boutiques discount stores department stores
Bridge	intrinsic value moderate prices fashionable	less expensive gemstones synthetic gemstones	silver gold plated gold filled light-weight gold	ranges from affordable to moderately expensive	department stores boutiques specialty stores some fine jewelry stores discount jewelry stores
Fine	long-lasting investment value timeless design	natural expensive gemstones	gold platinum	expensive	fine jewelry stores fine jewelry section of some department stores

7 *Buying Gemstones*

How knowledgeable are you about gemstones? Consider this true story.

Mary and a friend decided to go to one of the largest rummage sales in their area. While picking through the jewelry, Mary came across a strand of opalescent beads. At first glance, they didn't appear to be much — the clasp was broken at one end and the other end was frayed. As she looked at them more closely, however, the beads themselves looked very beautiful. Not being a jeweler or gemologist, she couldn't tell by sight whether they might be pearls.

She did know that "real" pearls could be differentiated from fake ones by a simple "tooth test." She knew that if she rubbed real pearls against her teeth, they would feel gritty. Fake ones, on the other hand, would feel smooth. So Mary rubbed the pearls against her teeth. To her surprise, they felt gritty. Encouraged, she paid for the 75-cent strand along with the other "bargains" she had found that day.

A week later Mary took the strand to her jeweler, who pronounced them fine, cultured pearls and appraised them at $1,500.

You may think you'll never get as lucky as Mary. But the point is that she wasn't the only one who looked at those pearls that day. She was, however, armed with information and knowledge about gemstones.

Being informed is a requisite of successfully shopping for gemstones, whether you're looking at them at a rummage sale or at Tiffany's. Gemstones are explainable and understandable, and to increase your knowledge about them doesn't diminish their allure or romance. Rather, knowing you made a purchase that was what you wanted and that was also a good value will add to the beauty of your stone.

WHAT IS A GEMSTONE?

The Latin word gemma *originally meant crystals.*

To be classified as a gemstone, a material must possess three qualities: beauty, rarity, and durability. Most gemstones are minerals. But, of the more than 3,000 mineral species that man has identified on the earth, only around 100 meet the three standards set out above and are traditionally known as gemstones. Beauty, rarity, and durability also permit other materials to be included as gemstones. Several of the most famous and most popular gemstones — pearls, amber, coral, ivory, and jet — are derived from living organisms.

Each of the three criteria for gemstones is based on distinct and measurable physical characteristics that determine the value of a gemstone. Beauty can be measured by evaluating the gem's color, clarity, and cut. Rarity is determined by the scarcity of the gem's occurrence in nature. And finally, durability is based on the gem's hardness, toughness, and stability.

Beauty

Color is the most important characteristics of gemstones.

Color: If one factor is most important in determining the value of a gemstone, it is color. Color accounts for approximately 60 percent of the gemstone's assessed quality. Even subtle color differences in a gemstone can make the difference in the stone being worth $10 or $1,000.

Judging the color quality of diamonds is made easier by an internationally accepted scale developed by the Gemological Institute of America (This scale is found on page 127). Judging the color quality of colored gemstones, all gemstones except diamonds, is much more difficult. However, with each colored gemstone there is a color of popular preference. This preferred color and how much a gemstone deviates from it directly affects not just the beauty, but also the value of the gemstone. In general, colors that are very light or very dark are worth less per carat.

The category of colored gemstones includes all gemstones except diamonds.

Clarity: As with many things that come from nature, gemstones are seldom perfect. They usually come to us with flaws or blemishes enclosed within — a speck of foreign material, a tiny gas bubble, a needle-looking crystal, a feathery edge. The surface of a gemstone can also be blemished with scratches, nicks, or abrasions.

In gemological terms, these imperfections are known as inclusions. A gemstone's relative freedom from inclusions is measured in terms of clarity. Clarity is a primary consideration in transparent, faceted gemstones, especially diamonds. Inclusions detract from the beauty and value of most gemstones, can impede the reflection of light through the stone, and, in some cases, even structurally weaken it.

Inclusions usually reduce the value of a gemstone.

You'll want to look for the presence of these dots, specks, bubbles, scratches, or other imperfections with the help of a loupe. This instrument, kept by all reputable jewelers, magnifies the gemstone a certain number of times, usually ten times. With that power, most inclusions become fairly obvious. And if they aren't, they're too tiny to be concerned about.

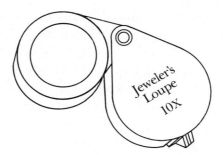

Another scale, developed by the GIA, helps to judge a diamond's clarity (see page 127). Again, there is no internationally accepted scale devised to rate the clarity of colored gemstones. But keeping the GIA scale in mind when evaluating the clarity of a colored stone can be helpful. Flawless colored stones are perhaps even rarer than flawless diamonds. In general, the fewer the inclusions, the more valuable the gemstone.

Cut: Until around the fourteenth century, gemstones were either carved or cut *en cabachon.* Cabachon comes from the French word meaning "head." It refers to the rounded top which is typical of this type of cut.

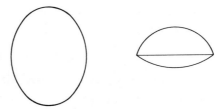

However, with the advent of modern cutting techniques, more sophisticated gemstone cuts were developed. These are the faceted cuts so popular today. Faceting is the placing of regular, flat surfaces on a gemstone in a preselected geometric pattern. For example, the most popular faceted cut, the brilliant cut, has fifty-seven such plains on each stone (fifty-eight if the bottom has a facet).

When cut properly, gemstones reflect light, color, and brilliance. In fact, a good cut can even conceal inclusions and show a weak color to its best effect. When cut improperly, gemstones are termed "dead," for they lack luster and sparkle and have their color washed out.

Rarity

Rarity is a hard characteristic to pin down. To command a high but still attainable value, a gemstone must be available enough to retain a share of the gemstone market. On the other hand, if a gemstone is too rare, few can own one.

Rarity is measured in two ways. The first is the rarity of the stone itself, the scarcity of its sources on the earth. For example, amethysts are arguably as beautiful as

THE DIFFERENCE BETWEEN A CARAT AND A KARAT

Carat (gemstones)

The international standard unit of measurement for gemstones. A carat is a measurement of weight, equal to .200 grams or approximately .007 of an ounce.

Karat (metals)

A measure of the fineness of gold equal to $\frac{1}{24}$ part pure gold. Fine (pure) gold is 24 karats. Other examples of lesser karatage are 18 karat, which is 18 parts pure gold and 6 parts other metal and 14 karat, which is 14 parts gold and 10 parts other metal.

emeralds, and they are actually more durable. But a 10-carat amethyst will cost thousands of dollars less than a 10-carat emerald because emeralds are not as abundant in nature. Rarity depends also on the size of the stones as they occur in nature. There is a tremendous price difference between a 3-carat sapphire and three 1-carat sapphires of the same quality, simply because 3-carat sapphires are much more rare than the smaller ones.

The standard unit of measurement for gemstones is the carat. It is a measurement of weight like pounds and ounces, only much less in amount. The word "carat" derives from the Greek word meaning "carob tree." Seeds from this tree were so uniform in weight that ancients used them as a standard for measuring gemstones. Around the first of this century a carat was standardized as ⅕ of a gram, or about .007 of an ounce, to use familiar terms. You can get an idea how small this unit of weight is by comparing it to the weight of some familiar objects. For example, a penny weighs 12.8 carats, a bobby pin weighs 3 carats, and a plain wooden pencil weighs almost 26 carats.

Around the turn of the century Europe and America adopted the metric carat as the standard for measuring gemstones.

A penny weighs nearly 13 carats.

Because a 1-carat stone is a rather large stone (in the world of gemstones), the measurement of a carat is subdivided into 100 points. Comparing the values of points and carats, a gemstone that weighs 50 points also weighs ½ carat. One that weighs 25 points is ¼ carat. The terms are interchangeable, much as 50 cents and half a dollar are. However, the term points is generally used to refer to gemstones of less than one carat.

The Relative Size of Brilliant Cut Diamonds

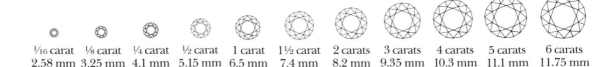

| ¹⁄₁₆ carat | ⅛ carat | ¼ carat | ½ carat | 1 carat | 1½ carat | 2 carats | 3 carats | 4 carats | 5 carats | 6 carats |
| 2.58 mm | 3.25 mm | 4.1 mm | 5.15 mm | 6.5 mm | 7.4 mm | 8.2 mm | 9.35 mm | 10.3 mm | 11.1 mm | 11.75 mm |

It's important to keep in mind that carat refers to weight, not size. And because gemstones are created from different materials, stones weighing the same will be different sizes. For example, a 1-carat diamond is larger than a 1-carat sapphire, but they both are smaller than a 1-carat emerald.

Mohs Hardness Scale

1	Easily scratched with fingernail Sulfur 1½–2
2	Scratched with fingernail Alabastor 2–2½ Amber 2–3 Ivory 2–4
3	Scratched with copper coin Pearls 3–4 Coral 3–4 Malachite 3½–4
4	Easily scratched with knife Rhodochrosite 4
5	Scratched with knife Lapis lazuli 5–6 Turquoise 5–6 Opal 5½–6½
6	Scratched with steel file Moonstone 6–6½ Kunzite 6–7 Tanzanite 6½–7 Peridot 6½–7 Zircon 6½–7½
7	Scratches window glass Citrine 7 Amethyst 7 Tourmaline 7–7½ Lolite 7–7½ Garnet 7–7½ Emerald 7½–8 Aquamarine 7½–8
8	Scratches window glass Spinel 8 Topaz 8 Alexandrite 8½
9	Scratches window glass Ruby 9 Sapphire 9
10	Scratches window glass Diamond 10

Durability

The durability of a gemstone generally refers to its ability to withstand ordinary wear. Durability is affected by three important factors: the gemstone's hardness, toughness, and stability.

Hardness: Hardness is a gemstone's resistance to scratching or abrasions. In the nineteenth century, a scale for measuring a gemstone's hardness was developed by an Austrian gemologist, Frederich Mohs. Mohs took ten well-known minerals and assigned them numbers according to their "scratchability." Called the Mohs Scale, and still used today, it ranges from 1 to 10. All gemstones fall somewhere between 10, the hardest (a diamond), and 1, the softest (talc). For comparison, your fingernail has a hardness of 2–3 and your fingernail file of around 5½.

Toughness: Understanding the difference between the terms hardness and toughness can be confusing at first. While hardness is a stone's resistance to scratching or abrasion, toughness measures a gem's resistance to breaking, chipping, or cracking. The old comparison between glass and plastic helps us to understand the difference. Glass is hard and resists scratching, but it is not tough. It breaks and chips easily. Plastic, however, is easily scratched but is very durable when it comes to chipping or breaking.

A gemstone's toughness is ranked as exceptional, excellent, good, fair, or poor. For example, while a diamond is the hardest material known, its toughness is only ranked as "good" because it is subject to chipping. A ruby, while less hard than a diamond, is actually tougher and ranked as "excellent."

Stability: This last factor measures a gemstone's resistance to attack by temperature, radiation (such as by the sun), and chemicals. For example, an emerald switched from extreme heat to cold can crack. Kunzite comes from the ground a bright pink, but if left in the sun will fade to an unappealing color. And pearls are susceptible to ruin from chemicals as common as hairspray.

Toughness measures a gemstone's resistance to breaking, chipping, or cracking. Some familiar gemstones and their toughness grade are:

Sapphire: excellent

Ruby: excellent

Amethyst: good

Coral: fair

Opal: poor

Emerald: poor

F ew gemstones will have it all when it comes to physical characteristics. A general order of importance when examining your gemstones is first beauty (color, clarity, cut), then rarity (size and rarity of the stone), and finally durability (hardness, toughness, and stability).

NATURAL, SYNTHETIC, AND ARTIFICIAL GEMSTONES

I n this age of technology, many things created in nature can be reproduced or at least imitated by man. It is no different with gemstones.

Because they have been duplicated and replicated, gemstones are divided into three classifications: natural (otherwise called genuine or mined), synthetic (also commonly called cultured or refined), and artificial (sometimes called simulated).

Each of these terms is referred to in this chapter. The Federal Trade Commission has issued some strict guidelines for the usage of these three words when applied to gemstone jewelry. (See 1979 FTC *Guides for the Jewelry Industry* for more information.) A *mined* or *natural* gemstone must come from nature. A *synthetic* is an exact recreation of nature's handiwork, having the same chemical and optical properties of the natural gemstone but created deliberately in a laboratory instead of accidentally in nature. *Artificial* only "looks like" a gemstone.

Natural, synthetic, or artificial stone—which one's for you? Any one or all three can be beautiful and fit your lifestyle. But because they differ greatly in value and price, you'll want to be sure of what you are getting. You won't want to pay for what you think is a natural emerald only to find that what you bought is more akin to bottle glass. Choose the type of stone you want—natural, synthetic, or artificial—then make sure you get it. If you are buying a natural stone, always ask for a certificate of authenticity of the gemstone.

When buying a natural gemstone, always ask for a certificate of authenticity.

ENHANCEMENTS

If the gemstone you're looking at is a natural one, you'll want to know whether it has been changed or treated. The gemological term for any alteration of a gemstone other than shaping it is enhancement.

Although there are many enhancements used on gemstones, seven are quite common: heating, irradiation, oiling, waxing, dyeing, bleaching, and lasering. Some gemstone treatments go back many centuries. The heating of sapphires and the oiling of emeralds are long-established enhancements. Others, like the lasering of diamonds, employ new techniques. Some are permanent, others are temporary. The table shown here describes each in detail, as listing the gemstones to which the treatment is commonly applied.

COMMON GEMSTONE ENHANCEMENTS

Method	Process	Gemstones commonly using enhancement	Permanence
Heating	using a high temperature to improve the appearance (usually color); may lighten, darken, or completely change the color	amber aquamarine citrine ruby sapphire tanzanite topaz tourmaline zircon	usually permanent
Irradiation	bombarding a gemstone with radiation to improve its color; sometimes used in conjunction with heat treatment	fancy-colored diamonds orange topaz blue topaz red tourmaline	usually permanent
Oiling	filling in fractures or cracks with a liquid oil (sometimes containing dyes) to improve color and mask the fractures	emerald	normally lasts for years
Waxing	filling fractures or spaces with a solid substance like wax or plastic	turquoise lapis lazuli opal	not permanent
Dyeing	using a chemical to darken an existing color or to make the color more evenly distributed	jade lapis lazuli opal pearl	can be attacked by chemicals
Bleaching	using a chemical to lighten or remove blemishes	pearl coral	permanent
Lasering	using a laser to lighten an inclusion	diamond	permanent

GEMS ABOUT TWENTY-FIVE
IMPORTANT GEMSTONES

O f the hundred materials classified as gemstones, many like talc, unakite, and ekanite are unfamiliar and seldom used in jewelry. For that reason, this chapter examines in depth only twenty-five of the most popular and important gemstones. Of those, diamonds, rubies, sapphires, emeralds, and pearls are dealt with first because of their premier importance and familiarity. The remaining twenty are presented in alphabetical order.

GEMSTONES FOUND IN THE UNITED STATES

Alaska
ivory
nephrite
rhodonite

Arizona
garnet
peridot
turquoise

Arkansas
diamond

California
amethyst
aquamarine
axinite
benitoite
lapis
morganite
nephrite
rhodonite

sphene
spodumene
topaz
tourmaline
turquoise

Colorado
lapis
rhodochrosite
rhodonite
topaz

Hawaii
coral

Idaho
aquamarine
garnet
opal

Maine
amethyst
apatite

morganite
tourmaline

Montana
sapphire

Nevada
opal
turquoise

New Hampshire
topaz

New Mexico
moonstone
peridot
turquoise

New York
amethyst
diopside
moonstone

North Carolina
aquamarine
emerald
garnet
ruby
sapphire
spodumene

Oregon
labradorite

South Carolina
amethyst

South Dakota
andalusite
spodumene

Texas
amethyst
topaz

Utah
red beryl
topaz

Vermont
garnet

Virginia
amethyst
garnet
moonstone

Washington
nephrite

Wyoming
nephrite

DIAMOND

A six-pointed diamond, pure, without stain, with pronounced and sharp edges, of a beautiful shade, light, with well-formed facets, without defects, illuminating space with its fire and with the reflection of the rainbow, a diamond of this kind is not easy to find in all the earth.

—Hindu gem-treatise

Kissing your hand may make you feel very, very good, but a diamond and sapphire bracelet lasts forever.

—Anita Loos, *Gentlemen Prefer Blondes*

Strange as it may seem now, diamonds once occupied a distant second place to colored gemstones in popularity for jewelry. Trouble was, the art of gem-cutting wasn't advanced enough to facet gemstones and, as a result, the diamond's fire, brilliance, and beauty was hidden beneath a lackluster exterior. Until faceting was mastered, colored gemstones offered a much more beautiful appearance.

Times changed. Around 1300, the technique for faceting gemstones began to be perfected by gem cutters in Europe. Diamonds were the first gemstone to be routinely faceted. Today, diamonds are the most important gemstone in the United States.

Once, all gem-quality diamonds came from India. But early in the eighteenth century, diamonds began to be mined in Brazil. That location became an important source for them. Then, in 1866, a young boy playing along the Orange River in South Africa picked up a bright and unusual pebble and took it home. It was in fact a 21-carat diamond, and it marked the beginning of the dominance of South Africa in the diamond market.

Today, South Africa remains the world's primary source for diamonds. Other major producers are the Soviet Union, Angola, Zaire, Sierra Leone. Recently, a deposit of diamonds including a number of "fancy" pink-colored diamonds was discovered in western Australia, and that country now holds a key position in the market.

Of all the diamonds mined, only about 20 percent are of gem quality. The remainder are used in industry.

Evaluating Diamonds for You

Birthstone: April

Hardness: 10

Durability and Wearability: Although diamonds are the hardest of gemstones and are suitable for everyday wear and enjoyment, they are not indestructible. Since they can crack and chip, diamonds should be removed when you're going to be very active or engaged in some activity that might result in the jewelry being knocked or abused.

Color: Diamonds vary from colorless to black. With the exception of a group of diamonds termed *fancy-colored diamonds* (those that are blue, green, pink, violet, red, or yellow), the colorless diamond is the most valuable. Thus, the value of color in a diamond involves how much the color varies from "colorless."

Because of the diamond's premier importance as a gemstone, the Gemological Institute of America developed a useful scale for assessing the quality of a diamond's color. This scale ranks diamonds from D the highest (colorless) to Z (a distinct evidence of yellow).

Color-grading Scale

D	E	F	G	H	I	J	K	L	M	N	O	P	Q	R	S	T	U	V	W	X	Y	Z
Colorless			Near Colorless				Faint Yellow			Very Light Yellow					Light Yellow							Fancy Yellow

Fancy-colored diamonds are extremely rare and costly. For example, a 3-carat blue diamond recently sold at auction for nearly three-quarters of a million dollars. Fancy-colored diamonds occur in browns and yellows (the two most common colors), also in blues, reds, pinks, and greens (the most rare).

Diamonds with poor color will often look yellowish. However, the distinct and intense canary yellow diamonds are termed fancy-colored diamonds.

Clarity: Because a diamond is basically colorless, the number and size of inclusions within the stone take on special importance. The GIA scale grades the value of a diamond according to the number and size of its inclusions.

Clarity-grading Scale

F	IF	VVS$_1$	VVS$_2$	VS$_1$	VS$_2$	SI$_1$	SI$_2$	I$_1$	I$_2$	I$_3$
Flawless	Internally Flawless	Very Very Slight		Very Slight		Slight Included		Imperfect		

Consumer Tips: Diamonds look best under artificial light. To more accurately assess any you are considering, look at three or four of varying quality. Then compare their color, brilliance, and fire under natural light and artificial light.

Because diamonds occupy such a prominent place in American lifestyles, it is especially important to know what you are getting when you buy them. The GIA scale can help you get a point of reference for color and clarity of any diamond you are considering. Ratings such as "Triple AAA" or "Superior" used by individual jewelers are not very meaningful unless you have a way to compare them to a standard such as the one used by the GIA.

When buying a diamond, be sure you get a certificate stating the exact weight of the diamond you are buying, not a "spread" of plus or minus two or three points. Such "spreads" almost never come out in your favor. A 47-point diamond is not a half carat. And if you are paying for a half carat and buying a 47-point diamond, you are paying more than it's worth.

You should also note the difference between the *total weight* of a piece of jewelry and the weight of a major stone in the piece. Anything described with total weight takes into account the carat weight of each diamond in the piece. A ring that is made up of three diamonds—a large center one of 1 carat and two others of ½ carat—may be described as "a 2-carat diamond ring." A more accurate description would be "the weight of the center stone is 1 carat, with two side stones weighing ½ carat each for a total weight of 2 carats."

Finally, if you are one of those in the market for fancy-colored diamonds, be especially wary of green diamonds. It is possible they have been irradiated (bombarded with nuclear energy) to obtain that special color. If so, it is a distinct possibility that the color will fade in time.

RUBY

The price of Wisdom is above rubies.
— Book of Job

Named the "Lord of Gems" by ancient Hindus, rubies are much more rare and costly than diamonds of the same size and quality. Both rubies and sapphires are of the same mineral species, corundum, and are identical in all characteristics except color. Rubies are the red or purple-red variety of corundum. In fact, rubies get their name from the Latin word for "red." All other colors of corundum are called sapphires.

Throughout history, rubies have always held a high place of honor in the world of gemstones. When he returned to Europe, Marco Polo related a story about a man who owned a ruby four inches long and as thick as a man's finger. For this one stone the emperor of China offered an entire city in trade. The owner refused!

It is the custom in many countries to give a colored gemstone as an engagement ring, primarily a ruby, sapphire, or emerald.

The finest rubies have always come from Burma. However, since the socialization of that country in the 1960s, few rubies are mined and sold through the government-regulated sale, and most Burmese rubies for sale today have been smuggled across the border into Thailand. Other important sources of gem rubies are Sri Lanka (Ceylon), Thailand, Kampuchea (Cambodia), Kenya, and Australia.

A few rubies (and sapphires) have phenomenal effects when cut *en cabachon*. During the formation of these rare stones, small needlelike inclusions occurred. When cut properly, these inclusions form a star. The effect is known as *asterism*, or the *star effect*, and the stone will appear to have a white star radiating from within. Typically, the star has six rays. Called star rubies or star sapphires, these are extremely rare and costly gemstones. Asterism is rarer in rubies than in sapphires.

In rubies (and sapphires) inclusions can be an advantage — they produce the phenomenal effect known as asterism.

Evaluating Rubies for You

Birthstone: July

Hardness: 9

Durability and Wearability: Rubies are extremely durable gemstones and wear well in all types of jewelry.

Color: The most prized and most valuable color of ruby is known as "pigeon's blood" red — a bright, clear red, with just a hint of blue. Violet-red colored rubies, though still beautiful, command far less value than the bright red ones. If the color gets too pale, they are no longer rubies but pink sapphires and are less valuable.

Clarity: Traditionally, rubies have more inclusions than diamonds. But, because the primary attraction and beauty of a ruby lies in its color, inclusions do not weigh as importantly in the value of a ruby as they do in a diamond. Still, they are a factor that should be considered. Any ruby should be eye-clean; that is, without inclusions evident to the naked eye. A lack of any inclusions in a ruby can often signal that the stone is synthetic.

Consumer Tips: Synthetic rubies have been available since the nineteenth century. When considering the purchase of ruby jewelry, especially at estate auctions and special sales, be aware that the ruby might be synthetic. The question isn't whether a mined ruby is preferable; either a mined or a synthetic may be what you want in a gemstone. The problem is that sometimes synthetics are misrepresented as natural gemstones.

Often the absence of inclusions flags a synthetic stone. However, eye examinations with a loupe cannot tell the difference. Only a gemologist who has special, sophisticated equipment can tell for sure.

Rubies can be color zoned. Color zoning in a stone is a band of light color adjacent to a band of darker color, thus resulting in an uneven distribution of color throughout the stone. It can detract from the color of a stone and lower its price and value. Often color zoning can be detected if you turn the stone over. However, a good cut will often reduce any detracting effects of color zoning.

Color Zoning

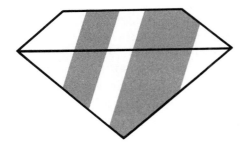

SAPPHIRE

To many people, sapphires mean blue gemstones. The word sapphire actually comes from the Latin word *sapphirus* meaning "blue." However, this gemstone comes in a rainbow of colors ranging from yellow to black, with shades like pink, purple, and green in between. Sapphires are often referred to with the color preceding the name, i.e., blue sapphire, pink sapphire. The orange-pink variety, however, has a special name — padparadschah.

The most famous sapphires come from the Kashmir district of India. Other important sources are Sri Lanka (Ceylon), Australia, and Burma. Gem sapphires are mined in the United States in North Carolina and Montana. The mines near Yogo Gulch, Montana, usually yield a fine blue color.

When cut *en cabochon*, sapphires, like rubies, can display asterism, the star effect. To judge the quality of a star sapphire, be sure that the star has all of its six rays, that the rays are straight, and that the star is centered on the stone.

Legend records that the Ten Commandments were written on tablets of sapphires. Ancients, too, credited sapphires with medicinal properties: it could protect against snake bites, remove foreign bodies from the eye, and act as an antidote for poison.

Always a popular gemstone, sapphires have recently gained even more prominence, boosted in part when Prince Charles chose a 6-carat sapphire for Diana's engagement ring.

Evaluating Sapphires for You

Birthstone: September

Hardness: 9

Durability and Wearability: Like its sister stone, the ruby, a sapphire is an extremely tough and durable gemstone. It wears well in any type of jewelry and is tough enough to be set in rings that take a fair amount of abuse.

Color: The preferred color of blue sapphires is a "cornflower" blue, a velvety blue color that doesn't fade to black under artificial light. The finest blue sapphires come from the Kashmir region of India and are found almost exclusively in estate jewelry because the mines in Kashmir haven't been worked, except sporadically, for years. Other fine quality sapphires come from Sri Lanka (Ceylon) or Burma. Australian sapphires are generally darker in color; those found in Montana sometimes have a metallic color of blue.

Sapphires in colors other than the familiar blue are called "fancy" sapphires. This term describes any other color but red (which is ruby). When judging the color of fancy sapphires, like pink, golden, green, or purple, their color should have a bright, robust intensity.

Coloration in sapphires can be uneven or zoned. Just as with rubies, turn over any loose sapphire you are considering on a diffused light source (tissue paper works well). Look at the back of it for evidence of a light color zone next to a dark one. Although a good cut can reduce the effect of color zoning, this does decrease the value of the stone.

If you are buying a fancy-colored sapphire like a pink or golden, be aware that inclusions are much more noticeable in these lighter colored sapphires.

Clarity: Expect to find inclusions in most sapphires, as you would in rubies. Large, visible inclusions, however, will reduce the value of a stone. In any stone, the fewer the inclusions, the better.

Consumer Tips: Sapphires also have been synthesized in the laboratory since the nineteenth century. Synthetic stones offer sapphires with the exact same chemical properties of those mined, except the synthetic stones were created in a laboratory and not by nature. If you're looking at a sapphire at an estate auction, be forewarned. Don't assume that because the stone is set in an antique setting it is a natural sapphire. If a natural sapphire is what you want and a certificate of authenticity is not available, you'll have to take the stone to a trained gemologist who has the equipment to tell the difference.

If you are buying a sapphire or any gemstone as an investment, to increase your chances of selling it or trading up, buy at least one carat. After that, select a stone with better color and fewer flaws.

WEDDING ANNIVERSARY STONES

1st	Peridot	11th	Yellow Zircon	25th	Green Garnet
2nd	Red Garnet	12th	Opal	30th	Pearl
3rd	Jade	13th	Hawk's-eye	35th	Emerald
4th	Blue Zircon	14th	Bloodstone	40th	Ruby
5th	Kunzite	15th	Alexandrite	45th	Cat's Eye
6th	Turquoise	16th	Red Spinel	50th	Golden Topaz
7th	Golden Beryl	17th	Carnelian	60th	Star Ruby
8th	Tanzanite	18th	Aquamarine	65th	Blue Spinel
9th	Green Spinel	19th	Almandine Garnet	70th	Smokey Topaz
10th	Blue Sapphire	20th	Golden Diamond	75th	Diamond

EMERALD

*No stone has a color that is more delightful to the eye . . .
neither sunshine, shade, nor artificial light effects any change
in its appearance; it has always a softened and graduated
brilliancy.*   — Pliny the Elder

Prized throughout the centuries for their brilliant
green color, emeralds today still retain that special
status. Along with rubies, they rank as the rarest and
most costly of all gemstones.

For some time, all green gemstones were called
emeralds. Julius Caesar collected emeralds because he
thought them a preventative for epilepsy and eye disease.
Other ancients believed they made their owners
clairvoyant. And because of their soothing color,
emeralds were believed to be beneficial to the eye. Nero,
it is said, watched gladiator combats through glasses
made of emeralds; lapidaries (colored-stone cutters)
routinely kept an emerald at their table to gaze into
when their eyes tired from work.

*The name emerald comes
from the Greek
"smaragdos" meaning
green stone. For some time
all green stones were called
emeralds.*

Although the most famous emerald mines of antiquity
were found in Egypt, worked extensively no doubt
because of Cleopatra's insatiable passion for the
gemstone, the finest emeralds were discovered centuries
later in Colombia by the Spanish conquistadors. Because
of their rich, deep color, Colombian emeralds are the
finest available. Other gem-quality emerald sources
include the Soviet Union and Brazil. Discoveries of
emeralds in Zimbabwe in the 1950s and more recently
in Zambia in the 1970s have led these two countries to
become leading sources. In the United States, some
gem-quality emeralds are found in North Carolina.

Emeralds have little fire and brilliance, so they need, to be cut in such a way as to maximize their exceptional color. A type cut commonly used to display this color and also to protect the fragile emerald from blows and knocks has been given the name "emerald cut."

Emeralds of fine quality and large size are scarce. Matched stones of over ½ carat are exceedingly rare. Large, flawless emeralds are among the rarest of all gemstones.

Evaluating Emeralds for You

Birthstone: May

Hardness: 7½ – 8

Durability and Wearability: Emeralds are not a durable gemstone and great care should be exercised when wearing them. They chip and crack easily, and are sensitive to heat and sudden temperature changes. Don't bathe or do dishes with an emerald ring on.

Emeralds are commonly oiled to improve their color. Leaving an oiled gemstone in the light such as in a window sill when doing dishes, can dry up the oil and potentially ruin the gem's color.

Color: The preferred and most valuable color of emerald is an intense, deep green with a soft, velvety appearance, sometimes called the color of young, green grass. A stone this color, or relatively close to it, is more valuable, even with inclusions, than one that is pale-colored with few inclusions.

Clarity: Expect to find inclusions in emeralds, even ones that are visible to the unaided eye. In fact, the occurrence and unusual arrangement of inclusions in emeralds are so common, they have been given a name, *jardin*, French for "garden." The size and number of inclusions in emeralds make up one reason that the stone is so sensitive to heat. When heated, the inclusions can expand and fracture the stone.

Consumer Tips: You'll want to be sure whether your emerald has been oiled, because this form of gemstone treatment will affect the durability and wearability of your stone. Oiling can usually be detected with an ultraviolet light.

   Emeralds, like rubies and sapphires, have been synthesized. In fact an inclusion-free emerald is so rare, you may well suspect it is synthetic. Synthesized stones are quite beautiful and cost thousands of dollars less than natural ones of comparable quality. Some women are switching to them for these reasons. The only disappointment comes when a synthetic stone is misrepresented as a natural one. If you are in the market for a mined emerald, beware of bargains and also emeralds set in antique jewelry. If a certificate of authenticity is unavailable, the only way to know whether the stone is genuine or synthetic is to have a trained gemologist check it.

A flawless emerald is very rare and usually found only in small sizes.

PEARLS

Because they come from nature essentially perfect and ready to wear, pearls are probably the oldest gemstone known to man. It is believed that pearls were worn and esteemed as long as 5,000 years ago.

Legend has it that Cleopatra won Marc Anthony's attentions when she crushed a large pearl worth nearly two million ounces of fine silver and drank it in a glass of wine at a banquet given in his honor. Constantine's helmet was covered with pearls. Roman women wore theirs to bed in order to insure sweet dreams.

At the turn of the century, pearls were so popular and so rare that a New York society matron traded her Fifth Avenue townhouse to Cartier for just a single strand of them.

Pearls are created when oysters secrete a substance called nacre around a foreign object that has entered their shells. There are two types of pearls: natural and cultured. Natural pearls form when the foreign object accidentally strays into the oyster. Cultured pearls form when man deliberately inserts the object (called a nucleus) into the oyster. Almost all pearls available for sale today are cultured pearls. Natural pearls are among the most scarce of gemstones, commanding prices of hundreds of thousands of dollars for a single strand.

Most pearls come from Japan, but some that are exceedingly large and uniquely colored (black, gray, golden-colored, blue, cream-colored) come from Tahiti, Australia, and Burma. Freshwater cultured pearls (often known as "Biwas" because most are grown in the Japanese lake of that name) feature strong colors (orange, pink, purple, blue) and have a "puffed rice" type of shape.

The value of a pearl depends on its luster, shape, color, and size.

Luster is the single most important factor in determining the value of a pearl. Luster is the deep-seated glow that sets pearls apart from other gemstones. Poor-quality pearls may reflect light off their surface, but good pearls glow from within. Luster results from the thickness of the nacre. The longer the pearl is left in the oyster, the thicker the nacre, and the more beautiful the luster of the pearl.

Pearls are the only "living" gems, having been created in a living organism.

In shape, the rounder the pearl, the more valuable it is. Irregular-shaped saltwater pearls, known as baroques, command only a half to two-thirds the price of round ones.

Pearls are measured in millimeters, a unit which approximates 1/25 of an inch. Average-sized pearls range from five to seven millimeters in diameter.

Pearls are measured in millimeters. Average-sized pearls range from 5 to 7 millimeters.

The colors of pearls vary, but each should be clean, free from spots, and should match the other pearls of the strand.

Evaluating Pearls for You

Birthstone: June

Hardness: 2½ – 4½

Durability and Wearability: Pearls are considered delicate gemstones. They scratch easily, and common household chemicals attack and pit their surface. Even cosmetics, hairspray, and perspiration can damage a pearl's surface. And once damaged, a pearl is ruined for life. Because pearls are so soft, avoid wearing rough fabrics that can scratch them.

Color: Pearl colors vary from white to black. The most familiar are the white or cream ones. However, other colors of pearls such as blue, gray, golden, pink, and black, do exist. They are much more rare and costly than the traditional cream-colored ones. Of the traditional cream-colored pearls, those with a subtle pink color overtone are the most valuable.

Clarity: In pearls, the quality of clarity is referred to as cleanliness or surface perfection. An occasional spot, blemish, or tiny pit is expected on something that comes from nature. Small blemishes are acceptable if they don't detract from the beauty of the pearl. Large, unsightly blemishes, however, substantially reduce the price of the strand.

Consumer Tips: *Faux* (French for "false") or simulated pearls are available in a wide range of materials, prices, and quality. Perhaps the best are Majorcan pearls — glass beads coated many times with ground fish scales. If you are not sure whether the beads you are considering are pearls or just good imitations, use the fool-proof tooth test: rub a pearl from the strand against a front tooth. Pearls that feel gritty are natural or cultured; those that feel smooth are imitations.

Judging pearls is easier than judging diamonds or other colored gemstones: with pearls, what you see is what you get.

To see if each of the pearls in a strand has been drilled through the center, roll the strand along a flat surface like the top of a desk. Any that haven't been drilled through the exact center wobble eccentrically.

Mabe pearls are large pearls that form like blisters against the inside of the oyster's shell. These, when filled in, make an affordable alternative to the traditional round pearls. They are usually larger and much less expensive. Because they form only a half sphere, they are commonly set in earrings or pins.

Pearl popularity tends to wax and wane with fashion. Some analysts connect the popularity of pearls with a conservative political administration!

TRADITIONAL BIRTHSTONE CALENDAR

January	Garnet
February	Amethyst
March	Aquamarine, Bloodstone
April	Diamond
May	Emerald
June	Pearl, Moonstone, Alexandrite
July	Ruby
August	Peridot, Sardonyx
September	Sapphire
October	Opal, Tourmaline
November	Topaz, Citrine
December	Turquoise, Blue Zircon

ALEXANDRITE

An alexandrite has a dual personality, possessing the remarkable characteristic of displaying two distinctly different colors: green in daylight, red in artificial light. Sometimes it is even called "emerald by day, ruby by night."

The color change phenomenon of alexandrite makes it appear green in daylight and then change to red at night.

Discovered in 1839, alexandrite is a relatively new stone in the world of gemstones. It was named for Russia's heir apparent, Alexander II, because it was supposedly discovered on his birthday. This, plus the fact that green and red formed the colors of the Russian Imperial Guard, made the stone a favorite with the Russian people. In fact, much of the fine alexandrite available today is found in antique jewelry that came from that country.

Alexandrite is far from abundant, very expensive, and rarely found in sizes larger than three carats. The Ural mountain deposit in Russia was mined out years ago. Today's sources are Sri Lanka (Ceylon), Zimbabwe (Rhodesia), Tanzania. A very recent deposit in Brazil has produced some high quality and larger stones.

Evaluating Alexandrites for You

Birthstone: June (alternate)

Hardness: 8½

Durability and Wearability: Despite its delicate colors, an alexandrite is a hard, durable gemstone, suitable for wearing in any type of jewelry.

Color: The finest stones change from green to red and vise versa depending on the light source. The most desirable colors are a brilliant grass green in daylight, turning to fiery raspberry red under artificial light.

Consumer Tips: Alexandrites are extremely rare and usually collector's items. Good quality stones should make a complete color change.

Be aware that there are many synthetic alexandrites on the market today, some of which were misrepresented as natural stones. When first produced, these synthetics were not easily identified. If you have a piece of alexandrite jewelry (most likely bought since 1973), it could have been mistaken for genuine. Again, only a trained gemologist can verify the authenticity.

AMBER

The price of a figurine in amber, however small, exceeded that of a living, healthy slave.

— Pliny the Elder

So wrote the great natural historian Pliny about amber's popularity in Roman times. Today, it still maintains this popularity.

Looking at amber is like getting a glimpse into prehistoric times. Amber was once pine resin. As it flowed down tree trunks, it trapped anything that lay in its path—leaves, twigs, insects, even small animals. These, unlike most inclusions, usually add to the value of amber. Over the passing centuries, this resin hardened into a soft and lustrous gemstone, amber.

The ancient Greeks thought amber was solidified rays of sunshine. It was so in demand, the Phoenicians opened new trade routes to its sources in the Baltic Sea to obtain it. Rosary beads during the Middle Ages were often made from amber.

For centuries, the primary source for amber was the Baltic coast of the Soviet Union. This remains an important source today, along with the Dominican Republic and Tanzania.

Evaluating Amber for You

Hardness: 2 – 2½

Durability and Wearability: Because it is lightweight, amber makes a good stone for bead necklaces or large earrings. However, its softness makes it extremely susceptible to scratching; care should be taken not to wear it with rough fabrics.

The body's oils enhance its appearance. The more amber is worn, the more beautiful it becomes.

Color: Amber ranges from transparent to black in color; however, it is usually the yellow to orange range that is used in jewelry. Deep yellows and oranges with a hint of reddish-brown are more valuable.

Clarity: While clarity is prized in most gemstones, inclusions found in amber, especially those of flora or animal life, make the gemstone more valuable.

Consumer Tips: If you are not sure that the piece of amber you are considering is real amber or a good fake, place it in salt water. Genuine amber floats; most imitations sink.

AMETHYST

Catherine the Great of Russia was so fond of amethyst she sent thousands of workers to Siberia to find them. The Greeks believed amethyst could prevent drunkenness—indeed, the word from which it comes, *amethustos*, means "not drunken." During the Middle Ages, it was regarded as a sure-fire cure for headaches, homesickness, the gout, and a personal protection from "wylde beasties."

Amethyst is the most highly valued gemstone in the quartz family of minerals. During Catherine's time, the gemstone was very scarce and costly, and it remained so until the discovery of large deposits in South America near the end of the nineteenth century.

In addition to the Soviet Union, other important sources are Brazil, Uruguay, Madagascar, and Zambia. In the United States, gem-quality amethyst is found (in small quantities) in Montana, North Carolina, Maine, Texas, Virginia, Arizona, and California.

Evaluating Amethysts for You

Birthstone: February

Hardness: 7

Durability and Wearability: Despite its delicate colors, amethyst is both hard and tough. It wears well in all jewelry, including rings.

Up to the beginning of the nineteenth century, colored gemstones were used as medicines. Treatments using them generally involved one of these three procedures:

1) bringing them into proximity with the afflicted person

2) placing the gemstone on the afflicted part of the body

3) powdering and eating the stone.

Color: Colors of amethyst range from pale lilac to deep purple. A deep, intense medium-dark purple is the preferred color. Like rubies and sapphires, amethysts can be color zoned with bands of dark and light color in the same stone, resulting in an uneven distribution of color. This can reduce the beauty and value of a stone. To check any stone for color zoning, turn the stone over. Often a good cut can reduce any unsightly effects of color zoning.

Clarity: Inclusions within an amethyst should not be able to be seen by the unaided eye.

Consumer Tips: Although natural amethyst is available in large amounts and is an affordable gemstone, much synthetic amethyst is on the market today and unfortunately much of it is sold as genuine amethyst. A new test for synthetic amethyst makes it easy to spot; if you are in doubt, a gemologist can quickly discern the difference.

Be aware that some natural amethyst, if left in sunlight, will fade.

AQUAMARINE

Aquamarines derive their name from the words "aqua" and "marine," meaning "sea water." Although aquamarines come in colors ranging from nearly colorless to deep blue, the predominant color is one of the seas. Because of its color, in ancient times aquamarine was said to aid seafarers. The stone was also thought to bring its owner courage in times of war.

Twin sister to the emerald (they are both members of the same mineral family, beryl), the aquamarine possesses several important qualities the emerald does not. Aquamarine is far more durable, usually flawless, and is found in much larger crystals. These distinctions, plus its striking, yet subtle blue color, combine to make the gem widely popular.

The finest aquamarines come from Brazil, although they are found on every continent. Other important sources are the Soviet Union, Madagascar, and Sri Lanka (Ceylon). In the United States, aquamarines are found in California, Idaho, North Carolina, Maine, and Connecticut.

Aquamarines are generally cut with an emerald cut. Large crystals of this gemstone are common; the largest ever mined weighed 243 pounds.

Evaluating Aquamarines for You

Birthstone: March

Hardness: 7½

Durability and Wearability: Aquamarine is considered a durable gemstone—much more durable than the emerald—and can be set in jewelry that is worn daily. Its relative toughness allows it to be set in gem rings, even in solitaire settings.

Color: Aquamarines range from almost colorless to an intense blue. The ideal color is a limpid sea blue, sometimes described as a "Caribbean blue." As the blue tone darkens, the value of the aquamarine generally

The chemical structure of an aquamarine makes it about 75% lighter than a diamond. Therefore, a 1-carat aquamarine is larger in size and appearance than most people expect a 1-carat stone to look like.

increases. Very dark stones are quite rare and expensive. The presence of green or gray decreases the stone's value.

Clarity: Because aquamarines are light-colored, they should be eye-clean, having no flaws apparent to the naked eye.

Consumer Tips: The aquamarine is one of the few gemstones whose appearance improves in artificial light.

CITRINE

Citrine (pronounced sih-treen′) takes its name from the French word *citron* meaning "lemon," although often this gemstone's color is a shade of yellow other than lemon-yellow. Many times citrines are a pale to dark shade of sherry. Citrine is the yellow variety of quartz, sister to the purple variety, amethyst.

Because the color range of citrine is similar to that of topaz, sometimes citrines are called by confusing names— "citrine topaz," "quartz topaz," and "Madeira topaz." Some of this confusion stems from the fact that in ancient times many stones were collectively named one name: all blue stones were called sapphires, all were ruby red, all green emerald, and all yellow topaz.

People once carried citrines to protect against the plague, skin diseases, snake bites, and evil thoughts. In times past, citrine was a far more rare and costly gemstone. When enormous deposits of quartz were discovered in Brazil, both the amethyst and citrine fell in value. Today, citrine is an affordable gemstone.

Citrine occurs in large crystals; sizes of 10 carats or more are fairly common.

Most citrine comes from Brazil. Other producing countries are the Soviet Union and Spain. In the United States, citrine is found in North Carolina and California.

Evaluating Citrines for You

Birthstone: November (alternate)

Hardness: 7

Durability and Wearability: Citrine is a hard and durable stone suitable for daily wear, even in a gem ring setting.

The "earth" tones of citrine complement many wardrobes.

Color: Citrines range in color from yellow to red-orange and orange-brown. In the past the "Maderias"—dark wine-red stones—were more popular and commanded higher prices. Today, however, the preferred colors are vivid yellows and oranges. Citrines can have color zoning. To check for this, turn the stone over. Any color zoning will be evident to your unaided eye.

Clarity: Citrines, because of their light color and abundance, should be free from inclusions visible to the unaided eye.

Consumer Tips: Citrine is an extremely affordable gemstone. A combination the two gems amethyst and citrine has been found in Brazil. Called "ametrine," the purple portion is bright and the yellow is a golden color. These stones are unique and relatively abundant.

CORAL

Coral, like pearls, is an organic gemstone found in the sea. It is a result of the life cycle of tiny animals whose calcified skeletons form branches on the ocean floor. The finest coral comes from the Mediterranean Sea, which is also the most ancient source for this gemstone. Japan, China, Vietnam, and the Hawaiian Islands are more recent sources. Black coral is found in Australia and the Red Sea.

As a gemstone, coral has occupied an important role throughout history. Ancients credited it with strong, curative powers; Roman parents hung branches of coral around their children's necks to protect them from danger. Romans also believed that a dog's collar set with coral would prevent rabies. In the United States, the Indians of the Southwest traded with the Spaniards for coral to use in their jewelry. Many antique Indian pieces using coral and silver still can be found in the southwestern United States.

Evaluating Coral for You

Hardness: 3–4

Durability and Wearability: Coral's hardness ranks low on the Mohs scale. It scratches easily; if worn with rough, scratchy fabrics, it can abrade.

Color: Although a rainbow's spectrum of colors are available in coral, white is the most common color and red is the most valuable color. The most sought-after color is known as "ox-blood" coral, a red that is uniform, strong, and bright. Pink and paler-colored coral, sometimes known as "angel's skin," is also popular, rare, and expensive. The golden and black colors are popular, too.

Consumer Tips: Coral is sensitive to heat, acids, and hot solutions. Its color can fade when worn. There are many inexpensive imitations for coral on the market today. The most common are made from glass, horn, or plastics.

GARNET

Asians once used garnets as bullets in the belief that their blood-red color would seek the blood of the enemy and therefore inflict a deadly wound. What these warriors didn't know, as well as a lot of people today don't know, is that garnets aren't just red stones. They occur in a variety of colors other than red—for example, green, orange, yellow, brown, purple. In fact, garnets come in every color except blue. Two of the most beautiful and expensive garnet varieties, the demantoid and tsavorite, are green. And the popular rhodolite garnets are a deep pink to purple in color.

According to ancient legend, the only light in Noah's Ark was provided by an enormous red garnet.

Although garnets are among the most ancient of gemstones, some varieties of it rank as recent discoveries. The grass green tsavorites, whose color rivals that of the emerald, was discovered in the 1970s. Garnets have always enjoyed popularity as a gemstone, but they reached the height of their popularity during the Victorian era, when the familiar red garnet was used in every aspect of jewelry.

Garnets are found in many countries. Major sources include Kenya, Madagascar, Sri Lanka (Ceylon),

Tanzania, and the Soviet Union. Some of the finest red-colored garnets are found in Czechoslovakia.

Evaluating Garnets for You

Birthstone: January

Hardness: 6½–7½

Durability and Wearability: All garnets are quite durable and can be worn easily set in any type of jewelry.

Although tsavorite garnets (grass green in color) are rarer than emeralds, they cost far less per carat.

Color: The preferred color of a garnet varies. In tsavorite garnets, the optimum color is a dark green; in rhodolite garnets, it is a deep pink. In both, a lighter color reduces the value of the gemstone. Of the most familiar red garnet, the blood-red color that resembles a ruby is the most valuable.

Clarity: Garnets should be eye-clean; that is, they should have no flaws or inclusions visible to the unaided eye.

Consumer Tips: Despite the fact that garnets are generally inexpensive, plentiful, and available, many artificial stones are used as substitutes for natural garnets, especially in "birthstone" jewelry.

IOLITE

Iolite (pronounced eye'-oh-lite) derives its name from its violet color—although it is more famous for its blue sapphire look-alike color than for its violet shade. Because iolite is modestly priced, at a few dollars per carat as compared to hundreds or thousands per carat for sapphires, it serves as an affordable, real gemstone substitute for the sapphire. In fact, it is often called by the misnomer, "water sapphire."

The Vikings appreciated this gemstone and learned how to use it. They found that by slicing it very thin, it would operate like a camera lens and filter out haze or mist, thereby making things clearer on days when the sun wasn't shining. Thus, by using iolite, Viking navigators were able to locate the sun and take their bearings even on hazy days.

Although ancient sources of this stone occurred near Viking settlements, in Greenland and Norway, today's main deposits include Sri Lanka (Ceylon), Burma, Brazil, and India. Iolite rarely occurs in sizes larger than a few carats.

Evaluating Iolite for You

Hardness: 7 – 7½

Durability and Wearability: Iolite is fairly tough and hard and can stand up to daily wear.

Color: Although iolite occurs in various hues of blue, some with violet tones, the preferred color resembles that of a blue sapphire.

Consumer Tip: Cut can make all the difference in the world to the color of iolite. If the cut is even slightly off, the color will gray.

Originally, names given many gemstones referred to the special characteristics of the stone. Most common were:

1) color
2) their place of discovery
3) their alleged mysterious powers.

JADE

Jade is actually the name used to describe two different gemstones: jadeite (pronounced jade′-ite) and nephrite (nef′-right). Often this is confusing, because both are well known as jade, but not by their mineral name. To add to this confusion, jadeite and nephrite look very much alike and are often used in jewelry interchangeably.

The name "jade" comes from the Spanish name for the gemstone, *piedra de hijada* or "stone of the loins." And the name nephrite comes from the Latin word meaning kidneys (ancients believed polished jade pebbles cured kidney ailments). Jade has always been thought to bring good luck and health. In the Orient today, this gemstone is still used as much for amulets as it is for adornment.

Burma is the only source of fine jadeite, most of it smuggled into Thailand. From Thailand the majority of today's jadeite is usually sent to Hong Kong, where it is fashioned. Nephrite is more abundant, found in New Zealand, China, and the Soviet Union.

Evaluating Jade for You

Hardness: 6½ – 7

Durability and Wearability: While a California earthquake ruined most every other piece in an art shop, the jade pieces, many of which fell from top shelves, were unharmed. Jade is the toughest gemstone — tougher than diamonds.

Color: Although jadeite and nephrite come in all colors,

the preference for jade is green, an emerald green shade.

Clarity: Jade stones should be semi-transparent and as inclusion-free as possible when illuminated from underneath with a light, like a flashlight.

Consumer Tips: Jade look-alikes abound. Dyes are frequently used to improve the color of jade. If you suspect dyeing has been used and want one that has not been dyed, only a gemologist can tell for sure.

KUNZITE

> *. . . one born in the United States should wear a gem from among those which our country furnishes.*
>
> —George Kunz, geologist for whom kunzite was named

When choosing loose stones, stay away from dark stones—they appear even darker when set.

Kunzite (pronounced koonts'-ite) is a product of the twentieth century, discovered in 1902 by a father and son exploring a California mine. That state was long thought to be the main source for this rare gemstone that ranges from pink to purple in color. Recently, however, it has been found in Brazil, Madagascar, and Burma. And even more recently, sources in Afghanistan have also been discovered.

Kunzite is a fragile gemstone and must be worn with care. It is often found in large sizes of 50 carats or more and usually needs to be cut in large sizes to show good color.

Evaluating Kunzite for You

Hardness: 6–7

Durability and Wearability: Kunzite is quite brittle and sensitive to knocks. For this reason, plus its relative softness, it is not suitable for a ring stone. Because sunlight will bleach its color, kunzite is better worn as an "evening stone." Also, avoid sudden temperature changes — the stone could crack.

Color: The beautiful colors of kunzite are some compensation for its brittle and fragile character. It ranges from a delicate pale pink to a deep blue-red. The preferred color is an intense, pink-violet shade.

Clarity: Kunzite's relatively light color shows any inclusions. Therefore, it should be eye-clean; that is, with no flaws or inclusions visible to the unaided eye.

Consumer Tips: Cut means everything to kunzite. A poor cut will haze the stone and rob it of its fire.

LAPIS LAZULI

Lapis lazuli (pronounced lap'-iss lazh'-u-lee) has been used in jewelry since the times of antiquity. So valued was it in ancient times that conquering armies would often list it ahead of gold when reporting booty captured. During the Middle Ages, it was ground up and used as a pigment for paint oils. It is thought that the Dutch painter Vermeer used lapis lazuli to create the distinctive blues for which he is so renowned. The Chinese named it "dark blue goldstone," which captures the look and feel of the stone.

The best lapis lazuli comes from Afghanistan. Some of the mines which produce high-quality lapis today have been in production there for some 6,000 years. Some lesser-quality lapis is mined in the Soviet Union and Chile. Small amounts are found in California.

Evaluating Lapis Lazuli for You

Hardness: 5–6

Durability and Wearability: Besides ranking as one of the softer gemstones and being subject to scratching and abrasion, lapis is also sensitive to pressure and high temperatures. However, it can be repolished if abraded.

Color: The preferred color of lapis lazuli is a uniform, deep blue without a hint of purple. Purple tones, as well as gray tones, reduce the value of lapis.

Clarity: Lapis is almost always opaque to semi-transparent and is usually cut *en cabochon*. White patches or the presence of any inclusions on the surface of the stone reduce the gem's value.

Consumer Tips: Some lapis is dyed to enhance its color. As the dyes used are unstable when exposed to even the most common household chemicals, such as perfumes, cosmetics, or perspiration, you should find out if the lapis you are considering has been dyed. Sometimes licking the stone and then wiping your tongue on a tissue will leave a telltale blue. There are many imitations of lapis on the market and some of these, which are glass or plastic, can look very real. Lapis is a favorite stone for men's jewelry.

To evaluate the cut of any stone, especially cabochons, imagine a line down the center. Is the left half symmetrical to the right half?

OPAL

The Roman Senator Nonius went into exile rather than part with his opal. Queen Victoria so favored them that she gave each of her daughters one as a wedding gift. Shakespeare called it the "queen of gems."

However, opals have been considered unlucky by some. Sir Walter Scott's heroine in *Anne of Geierstein,* Lady Hermoine, possessed a spooky one: it sparkled when she was happy, shot out red gleams when she was angry, and dissolved in a heap of gray ashes when she died. This story caught the public's fancy and unwittingly Scott perpetuated the superstition that opals are unlucky.

Actually, the opal's unlucky reputation probably stems from the stone setter's bench. It's a fragile stone — hard to set, easy to crack.

Opals are made up of tiny, gelled silica and contain as much as 20 to 30 percent water. Some opals dry out and crack (or craze), completely ruining the stone. Fortunately, most do this soon after being mined.

Yet opals are among the most beautiful of gemstones. What makes them special is the fiery play of color which changes with every movement of the gemstone. There are four kinds of gem opals.

White opal: a white or light background; the most common type opal found in jewelry.

Black opal: a gray, blue-gray, or black background; the most rare and valuable of opals.

Water opal: a transparent or colorless background; flashes of fire seem to swim in these. The colors generally found in these are purple, blue, and blue-green.

Fire opal: the background is more translucent and is red, reddish-orange, or reddish-yellow; these in general do not have the play of iridescent color the other three do.

Most opals are found in Australia, Mexico, Honduras, and the United States. The finest black opals are found in New South Wales at Lightning Ridge and White Cliffs. Before the turn of the century, the finest opals came from Czechoslovakia.

Evaluating Opals for You

Birthstone: October

Hardness: 5½–6½

Durability and Wearability: Opals are the softest of the more popular gemstones. They are brittle and sensitive to heat. Opals make a poor ring stone. If set in a ring, the setting should protect the stone.

Color: Black opals are the rarest and most valuable of opals. Because an opal's beauty depends on the contrast between the color play and the background, the darker the base color of black opals, the better. Also, the presence of red in a stone increases its appeal and value. The more green and blue increases, the less the stone is valued.

The best white opals display translucency and an interesting array of color. The finest show no identifiable

Three primary characteristics determine the value of opals:

1) the intensity of its colors
2) an even distribution of these colors
3) the actual color of the flashes in the opal; ranked in descending order of importance they are red, violet, orange, yellow, green, and blue.

background—just a continuous display of color pattern.

Consumer Tips: Opals often occur in nature in strips so thin, they can't be cut in regular cabochon stones. To utilize these strips in jewelry involves making composite stones, commonly known as doublets or triplets.

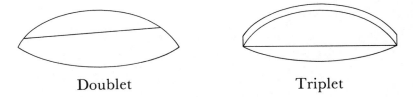

Doublet   Triplet

Doublets are a composite stone of two parts—a thin strip of opal mounted on a backing of some other material. Triplets are a composite stone of three parts—the same two parts of a doublet with a transparent top of quartz or some other colorless stone. Doublets and triplets cost much less than an opal and, if already mounted in a setting, are sometimes difficult to detect.

Black opals are quite rare. Costs of these are in the same price range as four of the most popular and commonly desired gemstones: diamonds, emeralds, sapphires, and rubies.

The most valuable white opals are cut in oval cabochon shapes with a strong curve to the cut.

PERIDOT

Once the pharaohs of Egypt prized peridot (pronounced pear'-ih-dot) so highly, they posted guards on their island source of this gemstone and gave them orders to kill any suspicious person attempting to come ashore. This ancient source, St. John's Island, is still known for the finest quality peridot, yet very little is mined there today. Peridot is mainly mined in Burma, Australia, Brazil, and Sri Lanka (Ceylon). A major source is the San Carlos Reservation in Arizona.

At its best, the color of peridot resembles that of an emerald, but it has more brilliance and sparkle. Cleopatra's vast emerald collection no doubt contained more than a few peridots masquerading as emeralds, because St. John's Island lay only thirty miles off the coast of Egypt.

A buying basic guideline for gemstones is: buy the best color you can.

In times past, peridot was often worn in earrings because it was believed it could make the faintest sound more audible. The gem was brought to Europe in great quantity by the Crusaders and became a popular stone for many ecclesiastical purposes.

Evaluating Peridot for You

Birthstone: August

Hardness: 6 – 7

Durability and Wearability: Peridot is a relatively soft gemstone, so cut peridot may lose its polish and become scratched over time. That plus its brittleness makes it a gemstone best set in jewelry not subjected to rough wear.

Color: Over the centuries, the prized color for peridot has been described as that of "the late summer green of grass." This color is difficult to find in smaller peridots, but the mass of larger stones intensifies its color. Most peridots have a trace of yellow in their green color; the more yellow, the less the stone's value. Dark olive green colors, those with brown in their color, are even less valuable.

Clarity: Clarity is extremely important when buying peridot. Inclusions give this lighter-colored stone a hazy appearance.

Consumer Tips: Peridot can be easily simulated with glass.

SPINEL

Two of the most prominent "rubies" in the British crown jewelry are really the gemstone spinel (pronounced spin-nel'). The 171-carat Black Prince's Ruby and the 361-carat Timur Ruby are both spinels.

Varieties of common spinel include almandine spinel (purplish-red), rubicelle (orange-red), balas ruby (rose-red), ruby spinel (red), and spinel sapphire (blue).

Indeed, if anything, spinel is a gemstone plagued by its similarity to other gemstones, especially the corundum family of sapphires and rubies. Red spinels look like rubies, pink spinels are often mistaken for pink sapphires, and blue spinels are often thought to be blue sapphires. The problem is compounded by the fact that spinels are found in the same two sources as sapphires and rubies, in Burma and Sri Lanka (Ceylon), and the spinel is usually found in the exact same gravel as corundum.

In addition to these two countries, spinel is also found in Afghanistan, Madagascar, Brazil, Thailand, India, Australia, and, in small quantities, in the United States.

Evaluating Spinel for You

Hardness: 8

Durability and Wearability: Spinel is a hard and tough gemstone, suitable for wearing in any type of jewelry. The blue variety is sensitive to high temperatures.

Color: Spinel occurs in all colors — red, pink, violet, yellow, orange, blue, dark green, black. The favorite and most valuable spinels are the red — possessing a color that approaches that of a ruby. Second in value and popularity is the intense deep pink shade that approaches that of a fine pink sapphire.

Clarity: Spinels tend to have fewer inclusions than rubies or sapphires and should look eye-clean, with no flaws or inclusions visible to the naked eye.

Consumer Tips: Spinels were among the first and the easiest gemstones to synthetize. Synthetic spinel has been available since the 1920s. It is often used in less expensive "birthstone" rings. Natural spinel is beautiful in its own right and can be purchased for about one-fifth the price of a ruby or sapphire.

Red spinel looks best in daylight and can fade into a brownish-red color under artificial lighting. For this reason, any spinel you consider buying should be viewed under different lighting conditions.

TANZANITE

In 1967 a prospector seeking rubies in Tanzania took a wrong turn. He stumbled onto a village where natives offered some soft, velvety blue gemstones he took to be sapphires. What in fact he discovered was a brand new gemstone — tanzanite (pronounced tan'-za-night).

It may be this century's answer for a gorgeous, blue gemstone. And tanzanite even features a wealth of valuable properties the sapphire doesn't. It often occurs in large crystals, is affordable, and, while it doesn't shine

After its discovery in the 1960s, tanzanite gained quick acceptance as an important gemstone.

GEMSTONES BY COLOR

Yellow
sapphire
citrine
topaz
amber
garnet

Orange
padparadscha (sapphire)
amber
topaz
tourmaline
zircon

Green
emerald
tsavorite garnet
demantoid garnet
alexandrite (by daylight)
peridot
tourmaline
jade

Pink
sapphire
coral
kunzite
topaz
tourmaline

Red
ruby
garnet (rubellite)
spinel
tourmaline
coral
zircon
alexandrite (under
      artificial light)

Blue
sapphire
tanzanite
spinel
topaz
aquamarine
iolite
zircon

Purple
amethyst
sapphire
garnet
spinel

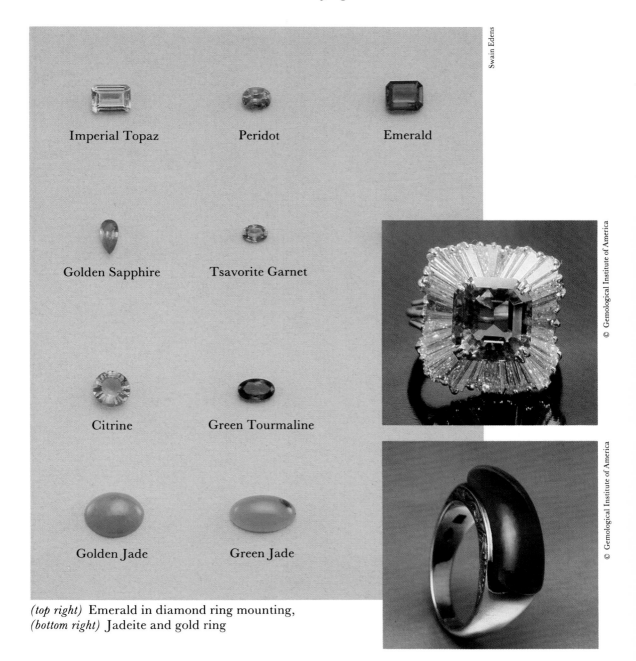

Swain Edens

© Gemological Institute of America

© Gemological Institute of America

Imperial Topaz

Peridot

Emerald

Golden Sapphire

Tsavorite Garnet

Citrine

Green Tourmaline

Golden Jade

Green Jade

(top right) Emerald in diamond ring mounting,
(bottom right) Jadeite and gold ring

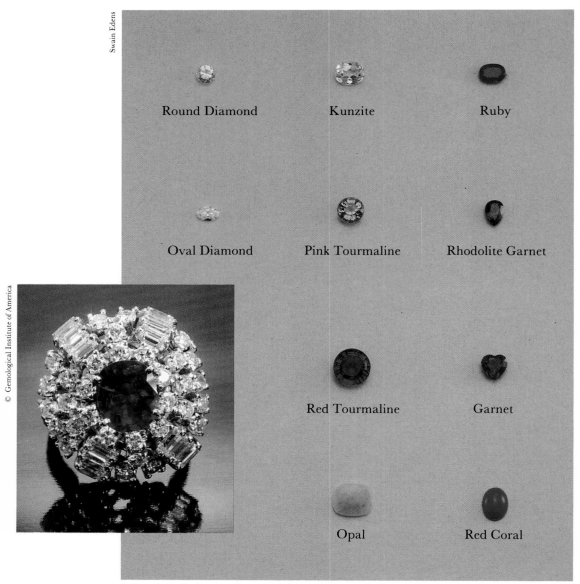

Swain Edens

© Gemological Institute of America

Round Diamond   Kunzite   Ruby

Oval Diamond   Pink Tourmaline   Rhodolite Garnet

Red Tourmaline   Garnet

Opal   Red Coral

(above left) Ruby in diamond ring mounting

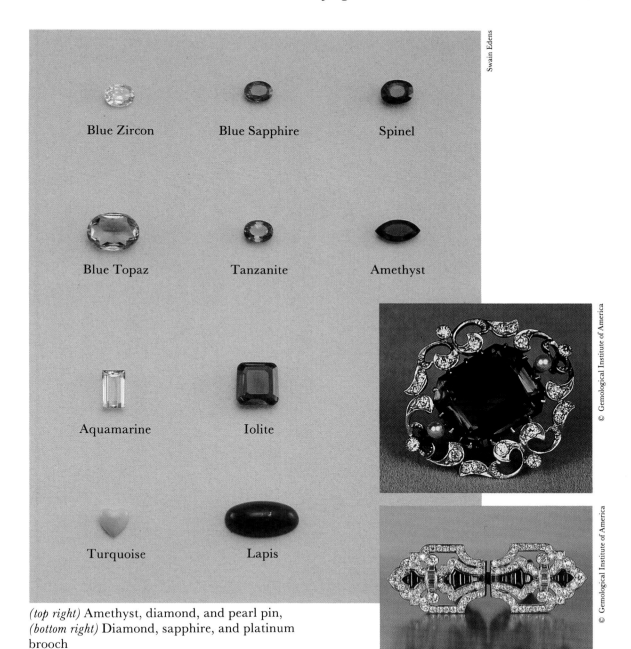

Swain Edens

Blue Zircon   Blue Sapphire   Spinel

Blue Topaz   Tanzanite   Amethyst

Aquamarine   Iolite

© Gemological Institute of America

Turquoise   Lapis

© Gemological Institute of America

(top right) Amethyst, diamond, and pearl pin,
(bottom right) Diamond, sapphire, and platinum
brooch

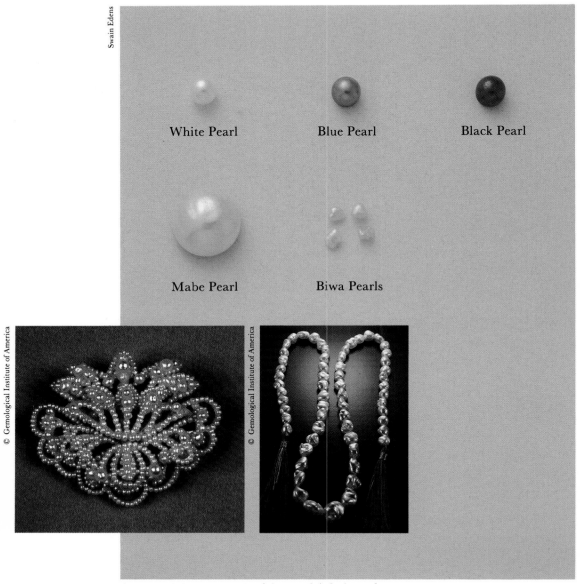

White Pearl   Blue Pearl   Black Pearl

Mabe Pearl   Biwa Pearls

(above left) Pearl brooch, *(above right)* Cultured
baroque pearls

brilliantly, it offers a rich, velvety, lustrous appearance. Tiffany and Company, first to introduce the gemstone in America, gave tanzanite its name, after the African country where it was found. As far as is known, tanzanite still occurs in only one source, Tanzania. It is seldom found in large crystals, stones above two carats being quite rare.

Evaluating Tanzanite for You

Hardness: 6½–7

Durability and Wearability: Tanzanite is as fragile and brittle as its delicate color would lead you to believe. Heat or sharp blows will fracture the stone. For these reasons, tanzanite is not a gemstone best set in a ring which is susceptible to blows and abrasions.

Color: Tanzanite ranges from a delicate violet to an intense, deep blue. The finest color is that of a velvety, cornflower blue—the ultimate blue for gemstones. A violet hue gives tanzanite a distinctive look and personality in its own right.

Clarity: Tanzanite as a rule has few inclusions and should be eye-clean.

Consumer Tips: Much fine-colored tanzanite has been heat-treated, which removes the undesirable green or yellowish tones. Heat-treating is permanent and does no damage to the stone.

Check the color of tanzanite in both daylight and incandescent lights. Some stones look faded when viewed under incandescent light.

Cut is especially important to a tanzanite; those cut improperly will look hazy.

TOPAZ

Don't buy gemstones when you are tired. Your color perceptions are not as clear.

Just as all red stones were once known as rubies, all blue stones as sapphires, and all green stones as emeralds, so all yellow or golden gemstones were once called topaz. The name topaz derives from the Sanskrit word *topas* meaning "fire."

But not all yellow stones are topaz and not all topaz is yellow. Topaz also occurs in red-brown, orange, blue, pink, red, lavender, and green. Most topaz found in nature is colorless, however. Because topaz is a lively, brilliant, and hard stone, in the past, colorless topaz was often confused with diamonds. The 1,680-carat topaz of the Portuguese Crown jewelry until very recently was thought to be a diamond.

Today's most important sources of topaz are Brazil, Sri Lanka (Ceylon), Burma, Russia, and Mexico. In the United States, it is found in New Hampshire, Texas, Colorado, and California. Medium to large stones are not at all rare. As were amethysts, garnets, and citrines, topaz was more valuable in years past than it is now.

Blue topaz, once extremely rare, is now the most readily available topaz on the market. Almost all blue topaz has been irradiated and then heat-treated, but this treatment is permanent.

Evaluating Topaz for You

Birthstone: November

Hardness: 8

Durability and Wearability: Although topaz is quite hard, it is a somewhat brittle gemstone and subject to fracture when hit by a sharp blow. Rings containing topaz should be worn with care. Avoid extreme heat when wearing, cleaning, or storing topaz.

Color: Traditionally, the finest topaz is sherry brown in color. In all other colors topaz comes in look for an intense deep color. The paler the stone, the less its value.

Clarity: Topaz should be eye-clean, free from any flaws readily apparent to the unaided eye.

Consumer Tips: Valuable topaz has a slightly velvety texture and a high luster. Citrine, a much less expensive gemstone, is often erroneously sold as topaz (unwittingly as well as unscrupulously). When compared to citrine, however, topaz is more brilliant and is a warmer color with a pink-orange tone.

TOURMALINE

The gemstone tourmaline (pronounced tour′-ma-leen) has something for everyone: it comes in a rainbow of colors; it is available enough to be moderately priced; and it is durable enough to be set and worn in any type of jewelry. All in all, the versatile tourmaline allows more options than any other gemstone.

Tourmaline allows more options than any other gemstone. Bicoloring or tricoloring is even found in a single gemstone.

As far as colors go, tourmalines have an array of more than 1,000 hues. But, unlike other gemstones, tourmalines can have two, three, or even four of these colors in a single stone. One of the most familiar is the watermelon—a mixture of a rich cherry red with a mint green. In fact, the name tourmaline derives from *turmali* a Singhalese term meaning "mixture."

Pink tourmalines are mined in California. So popular was this stone with the last empress of China that she ordered more than ten tons of it. Her mandarins wore pink tourmaline buttons. The first tourmaline Tiffany's bought came from Maine. Other modern sources are the Soviet Union, Sri Lanka (Ceylon), Burma, Madagascar, Tanzania, and Brazil.

Tourmalines have a long history of curative properties. Even today some are thought to be beneficial for healing. Dr. Jonas Salk has one.

Evaluating Tourmalines for You

Birthstone: October

Hardness: 7 – 7½

Durability and Wearability: Tourmalines are hard, durable gemstones that can be worn in any type of jewelry.

Color: The most valuable tourmalines, called rubellites, are red in color with just a tinge of purple. The presence of brown reduces the value of rubellites. The intense, shocking pink of California's pink tourmalines are also popular and valuable. The color of the tourmalines named chrome tourmalines and green tourmalines should resemble that of a fine emerald; chrome tourmalines, because of their rarity, are more valuable. Blue tourmalines are the most rare, and should be a bright blue or blue-green stone. Tourmalines that get too dark are less valuable.

Clarity: Like emeralds, tourmalines most frequently have inclusions. These internal characteristics can be proof of a natural or mined tourmaline as opposed to a synthetic or artificial stone.

Consumer Tips: Blue and green tourmalines in rich, deep colors are often used for men's jewelry.

TURQUOISE

Often regarded as a native American gemstone, the name turquoise actually means "Turkish stone." The ancient trade routes that first brought the gemstone to Europe came via Turkey.

Turquoise was one of the most valued stones of antiquity. Egyptians used it extensively and Aztecs prized it more highly than gold. In medieval times, turquoise was credited with having the power to protect the wearer from falls, especially falls from horseback. Turks often attached turquoise to the bridles of their horses as amulets. American Indians used it as a means of exchange and to adorn the fronts of their houses. To them, turquoise embodied the spirit of the sky and sea.

Today, the finest turquoise comes from Iran, but the major producing area is the southwestern United States (principally Arizona and New Mexico, with some mined in Colorado, Nevada, and California).

Evaluating Turquoise for You

Birthstone: December

Hardness: 5–6

Durability and Wearability: Turquoise is a soft gemstone and scratches easily. Heat, perspiration, oils, and cosmetics can cause an unsightly color change in turquoise. You should remove all turquoise jewelry before washing your hands.

Color: The preferred color of turquoise is an intense sky blue—one that is uniform in color. The paler the stone or the more green in its color, the less highly valued it is.

Clarity: Turquoise is opaque and much of it shows the presence of a matrix, a weblike threading of brown or gray through the gemstone. The presence of a matrix keeps the color from looking pure and reduces the value of the gemstone.

Consumer Tips: Although it is an abundant gemstone, turquoise is often treated or imitated. If you're in the market for the real thing, you will want to ascertain whether the turquoise you're considering is genuine and whether it has been dyed or waxed.

ZIRCON

The name zircon (zur´-con) probably derives from the Persian word *zargun* meaning "gold-colored," the color zircon occurs in nature. However, the zircon family of gemstones embraces a wide range of colors: yellow, brown, orange, red, violet, blue, green, as well as colorless. Hyacinth, which not only describes a type of zircon but also a flower, is the familiar red-yellow variety of this stone. During the Middle Ages, hyacinth was believed to promote riches as well as prevent plagues.

Because zircons have a high degree of fire and brilliance, they were once used as imitation diamonds. The most important sources for zircons are Vietnam, Thailand, and Kampuchea (Cambodia).

Evaluating Zircons for You

Birthstone: December (alternate)

Hardness: 7

Durability and Wearability: Zircons are brittle; hard blows or pressure will chip a zircon, especially on its faceted edges. For this reason, zircons are not a good stone to set in rings.

Color: With colorless zircons, the more whiteness and absence of color the better. The preferred color in blue zircons is an electric blue. The weaker the blue or the more green tone the stone contains, the less its appeal and value. The most important and valuable colors of zircons are colorless, golden-brown, and sky blue.

Clarity: Because zircons are transparent and generally light in color, they should be free from inclusions visible to the naked eye.

WHAT TO ASK WHEN BUYING A GEMSTONE

The following is a list of basic questions you should ask (or be told) before purchasing a gemstone.

1. Is this stone natural, synthetic, or artificial?

2. What is the carat weight of each of the stones in the piece? What is the total weight of all the stones if there is more than one?

3. Has this gemstone been treated or enhanced? If yes, what treatment was used and is it permanent?

4. What cut was used on this gemstone?

5. What are the major flaws in this stone?

6. If the stone is a diamond, where does it rank on the GIA scales for color and clarity? If another scale was used to rank it, how does that compare to the GIA scale?

7. If the cost warrants it, is this gemstone certified?

8. Are there any special care instructions for this gemstone?

Finally, make sure all these facts are recorded on your bill of sale.

COMMON GEMSTONE CUTS

Brilliant Full Cut

Eight Cut

Marquise Cut

Emerald Cut

Cabachon Cut

Baguette Cut

Antique Cut

Oval Cut

Pear-shaped Cut

Ceylon Cut

Heart-shaped Cut

Scissor Cut

8 *The Metals In Your Jewelry*

STERLING SILVER!
14-KARAT GOLD FILLED POST!
HEAVY GOLD ELECTROPLATE!
THE METAL OF THE SPACE AGE!

Familiar with ads like this? But confused as to what they mean?

Advertisements and signs at jewelry counters abound with phrases like these. But what are they telling you? Gold filled or karat gold, sterling silver or silver plate — exactly what is each? What are you really getting for the money you spend?

A key element in any piece of jewelry is the metal from which it is made. Building your knowledge about the metals in your jewelry is like constructing the foundation of a house: it will form a sturdy basis for all your jewelry purchases. Today, many jewelry pieces consist only of metal. Knowing about metals leads to successful and wise purchases.

Jewelry metals can be divided into three categories. The first, called the "noble" metals, consists of gold, silver, and platinum. "Noble" in character because they resist rust and corrosion, these three metals are also characterized by their rarity, intrinsic value, and expensive prices.

The second group of metals are called the "lesser" metals — those metals that corrode and tarnish easily, but are also more abundant in nature. In antiquity this was iron and copper, and the alloys made from copper. Today, the "lesser metals" has expanded to include many inexpensive metals that do not corrode, such as aluminum and pewter.

A third group of jewelry metals came into existence with the advent of the space age. A trio of modern-sounding metals make up this category: titanium, tantalum, and niobium. Each is lightweight and affordable.

THE NOBLE METALS

Gold

"The golden years" . . . "a heart of gold" . . . "golden anniversary" . . . "good as gold." Gold has come to be a standard of measure in our lives.

Four thousand years before the birth of Christ, man was seeking gold, using it for implements and adornment. The ancient Egyptians believed gold to be solidified fire. Tutankhamen's inner coffin was made of solid gold, forty-four pounds of it. So important was the possession of gold that many men of the Middle Ages spent their entire lives trying to change common metals into gold. Discovery of gold in 1849 led to a "rush" of American settlers to California and the settlement of our West. Today, space probes have located it on Mars, Mercury, and Venus.

Gold earns its exalted position. It is the most workable of all metals. One ounce of gold can be stretched into a wire 50 miles long or hammered into a sheet that covers 100 square feet. It is also the most durable and corrosion-proof metal. Gold sunk in shipwrecks is recovered in the same shiny condition it evidenced on the day it was lost.

Gold pebbles found in mountain streams or chunks dug out of mines are pure gold. This pure gold, however, is too soft — and too expensive — to be used in jewelry. Therefore, it is alloyed (mixed) with at least one other lesser metal to give it strength. The amount of gold in these alloys varies according to a system of karats devised centuries ago by Roman goldsmiths.

To see how the karat system works, look on any piece of solid gold jewelry you have. Somewhere on it, a karat marking must be stamped. That's the little mark on the inside of the ring band, bracelet clasp, or the back of the earrings that has a number from 1 to 24 followed by a symbol like "K" or "Kt." It will most likely read "10K," "12K," "14K," or "18K" because these are the most commonly used karat alloys.

If you had a piece of pure gold jewelry (which you probably won't because it is too soft and generally not made into jewelry), it would be marked "24K." Pure (fine) gold is 24K, or 100 percent gold. The number (1–24) tells you the number of parts, by weight, of pure gold that are in the piece.

For example, suppose you have on a gold ring marked "14K." This means that the mixture of the gold alloy is 14 parts pure gold and 10 parts other metals (to equal a total of 24 parts of fineness). Silver, copper, zinc, and nickel are the other metals commonly alloyed with gold.

In the United States, the karat system of fineness uses a scale of 1 to 24 to define the actual gold content of a gold alloy. In Europe, however, karatage is expressed in a scale which ranges from 1 to 1,000.

If you have a bracelet marked "18K," it consists of 18 parts pure gold mixed with 6 parts of another metal or metals. As you can see, 18-karat gold has a larger percent of pure gold in the alloy than a 14-karat piece.

Solid gold is not the same as pure gold. Solid gold simply means that the piece is not hollow inside.

According to government regulations, only 24-karat can be referred to as *pure gold*. The chart below can be used as a reference if you are buying karat gold pieces.

In the United States, ten-karat gold is the minimum legal standard . Interestingly, 9-karat is the minimum in Great Britain and Canada, while in France and Italy the minimum is 18-karat. This 18-karat is the highest karatage normally used in western countries. However, 22-karat is especially popular in the Orient.

FINENESS OF GOLD KARATS

Karat Marking	Karat Formula Gold + Other Metal = 24	% Gold	European Marking
24K	24 + 0 = 24	100%	999
18K	18 + 6 = 24	75%	750
14K	14 + 10 = 24	58.33%	585
12K	12 + 12 = 24	50%	500
10K	10 + 14 = 24	41.60%	–

As you found when examining your jewelry, any article of karat gold is marked with the amount of karatage. By law, the alloy amount (10, 12, 18, etc.) must precede the marking for karat, generally written "K." The following is a list of other acceptable marks for the "K":

Karat

Karat Gold

Kt

Kt Gold

K Gold

When a bracelet, ring, earrings or any piece of jewelry has such a quality mark, it also must have the firm's trademark or trade name stamped on the piece, as close to the karat marking as possible.

Alloying gold can be used to change its natural bright yellow color to other colors such as white, pink, or green. The formulas for creating colored golds can be seen in the table below.

COLOR	METALS USED IN ALLOY
yellow gold	gold, copper, silver
white gold	gold, nickel, zinc, copper
green gold	gold, silver, copper, zinc
pink or red gold	gold, copper

No matter the color, if a piece of jewelry is stamped with a karat marking (14K, 18K, etc.) it will contain that percentage of pure gold.

But what if karat gold prices exceed your budget?

In that case, you may want to consider gold platings or gold coatings. But a word of caution: there is a considerable difference between the types, methods, and qualities of the alternative.

Gold Filled (G.F.) Think of gold filled as a sandwich made from gold and another metal, called a base metal. At the manufacturing stage, a thick center of less costly metal called the base metal (usually brass or bronze) is sandwiched in between a layer of karat gold. The base metal and the karat gold covering are bound together using heat and pressure. Since the inside base metal is covered, gold filled gives the appearance of karat gold at a substantially reduced price.

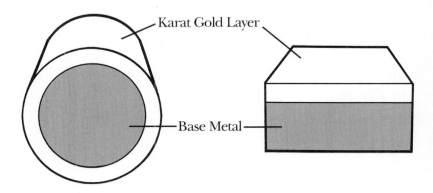

In all gold filled items, the weight of the karat gold layer must be at least $\frac{1}{20}$ or 5 percent of the total weight of the piece. This content, plus the karat fineness of the layer, is shown with a stamping such as:

$\frac{1}{20}$ 10K G.F.

or

$\frac{1}{10}$ 14K G.F.

Obviously, a piece stamped with the latter marking, $\frac{1}{10}$ 14K G.F., is superior, since it has a $\frac{1}{10}$ or 10 percent karat gold covering and that gold is 14-karat. In considering gold filled items, the greater the fraction and the karat number stamped on the piece, the thicker the layer of gold and the more durable the piece is. Because the weight of a karat gold layer must be at least $\frac{1}{20}$ of the total weight of the piece, this fraction can be omitted from the stamping. Therefore, sometimes you encounter gold filled jewelry marked:

12K G.F.

14K G.F.

The layer of karat gold that surrounds a gold filled piece of jewelry must be at least $\frac{1}{20}$ of the total weight of the piece.

In this case, the layer of gold is understood to be the $\frac{1}{20}$ standard.

Rolled Gold Plate (R.G.P.) Rolled gold plate is made by the same method as gold filled, except that rolled gold plate can have a weight ratio that is less than $\frac{1}{20}$. (The karat fineness must, as always in the United States, be 10K.) With rolled gold plate jewelry, the gold layers of the sandwich are thinner, so the jewelry is less expensive but less durable. Because there is no minimum weight standard, the fractional part of karat gold used in a piece must be stamped on each piece of rolled gold plate jewelry. For example, pieces may be stamped ¹⁄₄₀ 10K Rolled Plate ¹⁄₃₀ 12K R.G.P.

Gold Overlay Gold overlay is a term sometimes used for gold filled or for rolled gold plate.

Plaque D'or Lamine This term is the same as rolled gold plate.

The coating of gold electroplate must be at least ⁷⁄₁,₀₀₀,₀₀₀ of an inch thick.

Gold Electroplate This process, which is quicker and cheaper than gold filled, immerses a finished design or piece of jewelry made from a base metal like brass or bronze in an electrolytic solution. Tiny particles of karat gold in the solution bond to the surface of the piece. The particles build up, forming a thin film of gold over the design. To be stamped as "gold electroplate," this coating must reach a thickness of 7/1,000,000 of an inch and must be of 10K fineness. Thinner coatings of gold electroplate are called "gold tone," "gold flashed," or "gold washed." Gold electroplating is the cheapest way to give the appearance of karat gold.

Heavy Gold Electroplate This is the same method as gold electroplate, but heavy gold electroplate has a layer of 100/1,000,000 of an inch thick. Heavy gold electroplate is marked: H.G.E.

Vermeil Vermeil (pronounced vur-may′) is gold electroplating over a sterling silver base.

Gold Leaf Gold leaf is a very thin layer of gold used for gilding. It is laid over the surface of an object and then burnished (rubbed with a tool) into place. Gold leaf is so thin it is not commonly used in jewelry.

At first, comparing the two main processes of gold coating — gold filled and gold electroplating — seems a bit like comparing apples and oranges. The standard of gold filled is weight; the standard of gold electroplating is thickness. In general, though, gold filled will be thicker, more durable, and more expensive than gold electroplate.

Both, however, have a limitation. Gold is a soft metal and gold-coated jewelry can wear through and expose the base metal. The thinner the layer of gold coating, the sooner it wears through. When exposed to air, the base metal, usually brass or bronze, corrodes. Even the silver used in vermeil oxidizes when exposed.

The two main processes of gold coating are gold filled and gold electoplating.

GOLD BULLION COINS

Although the Romans were the first to use coins as jewelry, this fashion practice continues today. The chart below gives the most popular gold bullion coins used in jewelry, their karat fineness, weight, and percentage of gold.

COIN	TOTAL WT. (TROY OZ.)	KARAT FINENESS	% GOLD	DIAMETER
American Eagle 1986 to present	1.000	22	91.7%	34 mm
Canadian Maple Leaf 1979 to present	1.000	24	100%	30 mm
Mexican 50-Peso 1947	1.3346	21.6	90%	37 mm
Saint-Gaudens 1907 – 1933	1.0750	21.6	90%	34 mm
Krugerrand 1967 to present	1.0905	22	91.7%	32.3 mm
Chinese Panda 1982 to present	1.000	24	100%	32.05 mm

SILVER

Like pure gold, pure silver is too soft for most ordinary uses. So it too must be alloyed. In the case of silver, there is just one principal standard to be considered — that of sterling silver. This standard, of 92.5 percent silver and 7.5 percent parts of another metal, usually copper, was adopted in the fourteenth century by Henry II of England. For several years, immigrant German silversmiths had consistently refined quality silver for the English. These Germans were called "Easterlings" after the geographic area in which they settled. The product they made came to be known as E*asterling* silver, the "ea" eventually being dropped.

Like karat gold, pieces made of sterling silver are generally, but do not have to be, marked as such. The most common mark is "sterling." Other marks used are

sterling silver

silver

solid silver

The manufacturer's trademark should be as near the quality mark as possible.

Note that because there is only one standard of fineness for silver, no numbers are necessary. When an article is quality marked, the firm's trademark or trade name must be as close to the quality mark as possible.

Of the three precious metals, silver is the most lustrous, easiest to work, the least expensive, the most plentiful, and has a nice feel and texture (hence its use in table utensils). Yet, it has some disadvantages: when exposed to the air, sterling silver tarnishes; it is also less durable than gold or platinum.

In addition to sterling silver, you may encounter the following terms when you buy silver jewelry.

Mexican Silver Ironically, not all Mexican silver is made in Mexico. It is generally more pure than sterling silver, usually containing the ratio of 95 percent silver and 5 percent copper. However, Mexican silver can range from 90 percent to 99 percent pure silver.

Coin Silver This silver alloy of 90 percent silver and 10 percent copper was once the standard found in all United States silver coins. Because it contains less than 92.5 percent silver, it cannot be called sterling.

Silver Filled Silver filled is the silver version of gold filled. It, like gold filled, must have a coating of sterling silver that is at least $\frac{1}{20}$ the total weight of the piece.

Silverplate The process used to silverplate any article is the same as that used for gold electroplating: a coating of silver of at least 7/1,000,000 of an inch is deposited over a design or piece of jewelry made from a lesser metal like brass or bronze.

Nickel Silver Any piece of jewelry advertised as "nickel silver" contains *no* silver. Nickel silver is an alloy that looks silvery in color, but consists principally of nickel, copper, and zinc. It is often used in costume jewelry.

German Silver Like nickel silver, German silver is a misnomer. It contains *no* silver; it is an alloy of nickel, copper, and zinc often used in costume jewelry pieces.

Platinum

Spanish conquistadors tromping through the New World in the area of what is today Colombia came upon a silvery-looking metal the Indians used in their jewelry. It wasn't silver and the Spaniards considered it a nuisance. They tossed all they found into the water or caves to "age." In fact, they even gave this metal the name "platina" or "little silver" — meaning that it wasn't quite ready to be real silver.

This was platinum. Today, we know it as the noblest metal. Platinum is strong, nontarnishing, rare, and more costly than gold. It is the metal of choice for much fine jewelry.

Platinum commonly occurs in a group of six metals when it is found in nature. Known as the "platinum family," it contains, in addition to platinum: iridium, palladium, ruthenium, rhodium, and osmium. Iridium is commonly alloyed with platinum in a ratio of 10 percent iridium to 90 percent platinum to form the alloy with which most platinum jewelry is made.

THE LESSER METALS

Aluminum

In the decades after its discovery, aluminum was more prized and costly than gold. Today, it is a quite common metal often used in costume jewelry. Silvery-white in color, it takes a brilliant polish and can be combined with silver, copper, bronze, brass, and nickel.

Aluminum is lightweight, fairly inexpensive, very malleable, and resistant to oxidation.

Brass

Brass is an alloy of copper and zinc. Shiny brass resembles gold. Brass, however, tarnishes easily and some people react to it. Brass earwires should never be worn because they can cause serious infections.

Today, brass is used in pieces of jewelry such as inexpensive bangles and bracelets and is also found in many uniquely designed pieces of ethnic jewelry. It is frequently used as the foundation or base metal for gold-filled jewelry.

Bronze

Bronze is another common alloy of copper. Reddish-brown in color, it is made by combining tin and copper. Hard and durable, bronze takes a good polish and is often used in fashioning jewelry pieces as well as a base for enamels. It also serves as a base metal for platings and for enamels.

Copper

Copper was probably the first metal to be used by man — some 8,000 years ago. Today, copper is still widely used in jewelry. Lightweight and inexpensive, shiny copper looks like pink gold. It tarnishes quickly but can be restored to its original gleam with any of the commercial polishes found on the market. Copper is often used in inexpensive jewelry designs (mostly bangles and bracelets) and in original, ethnic designs. Its main use, however, is in making alloys for other metals.

Nickel

Nickel is commonly used in making precious metal alloys—white gold and sometimes sterling silver. It is the primary metal used in making "nickel silver," a metal used often in costume jewelry. It is hard, workable, nearly white, and inexpensive metal.

As much as 6 percent of the population is allergic to nickel. Because it is sometimes used in alloying sterling silver, often women who have an allergic reaction (usually with pierced earrings) assume that they're allergic to silver. If you can't wear some pieces of jewelry, it may be the nickel in the alloy.

Pewter

Once widely used, pewter fell into disrepute because it was alloyed with lead. Today, by law in the United States, pewter can contain no lead. Pewter is a silver-white metal, inexpensive, and easily shaped. Used primarily in tableware, it has recently gained acceptance in inexpensive modern jewelry.

SPACE AGE METALS

Titanium

A result of the search for strong, lightweight materials to be used in the space program, titanium has also found a niche in the jewelry world. In addition to being strong and lightweight, titanium can be colored by heating and displays a rainbow of brilliant colors which makes it a popular metal with the current fashion trend. Titanium is hypoallergenic, which makes it safe for most sensitive jewelry wearers.

Tantalum

Tantalum is dark gray in color but can be changed into a wide range of colors by heating. Of the three space age metals, tantalum is the most expensive. It is heavier than titanium and niobium. This extra weight gives it a more valuable feel. The major drawback of this metal is its softness.

Niobium

The most versatile of the three space age metals, niobium forms easily, is lightweight, and features a wide range of colors. It is more expensive than titanium — the price of it being on a par with silver — and is also hypoallergenic.

In jewelry today, almost any metal goes. In fact, combinations of metals are often used in designs — silver and gold, space age with traditional "noble" metals, combinations of the "lesser" metals. Each metal offers special properties, a special look, and gives a special feel to jewelry.

9
Organizing an Effective Jewelry Wardrobe

N ow it's time to look at *your* jewelry wardrobe. Time to gather all the pieces together — take the pins off your jacket lapels, retrieve the earrings from the bottom of your purse, and pull all the pieces out of your jewelry box. Lay everything out in front of you on a soft surface, such as a bedspread or a tablecloth, so your jewelry won't get scratched and you can see the collection in its entirety. It's time to determine what works and what doesn't, to discover and try new combinations as well as to rediscover pieces you might have forgotten.

A good idea is to begin assessing your collection's condition and workability by sorting out the pieces that are unwearable in their present state — bracelets with broken clasps, chains that have worn through their plated layer, single earrings, pieces with stones missing, unstrung beads. Since most women have been putting their jewelry collection together since high school days — or earlier — this may take quite some time.

After you've finished weeding out all these pieces, consider them for a minute. Are they repairable? And if they are, do you want to spend money you've budgeted for jewelry to have them fixed? Set aside all those pieces to which you've answered "yes." You can take them to be repaired on your next trip to the jeweler.

Deciding what to do with the remaining unrepairable pieces may take awhile. Jewelry isn't like clothes — what's not worn doesn't automatically go into a garage sale. It's virtually impossible to discard a 14K gold earring, even if its mate has been lost for ten years. It's also hard to throw away the shell necklace your husband bought you on your honeymoon, even though several of the shells are cracked.

One solution is to put this "memento" jewelry in a special place, apart from the jewelry you wear. Another solution is to sell the bent or broken pieces and odd earrings made of precious metal at scrap value and use this money to make new jewelry purchases. Some jewelry companies even allow you to trade these in on new purchases. For the unmatched, broken, or out-of-style gemstone pieces that you have, you may want to consider having the gemstones reset in a new design, one that matches your lifestyle and complements your special features.

Now, what about those pieces that you have just discovered don't do the most to flatter you? What should you do about the round silver ear clips that neither enhance your special coloring nor your facial shape? Or that long chain and pendant that only make your heart-shaped face seem longer and your chin sharper?

You may want to take a lesson from Shirley and Elaine, the sisters who traded jewelry to each's advantage in Chapter Two. Try trading jewelry with a sister, your mother, or a friend. They too may have some "mistakes" lying in the bottom of their jewelry box — "mistakes" that would look stunning on you, not to mention help complete your jewelry collection. And there's one distinct advantage to trading jewelry: it's much easier to fit than clothing.

INVENTORYING YOUR JEWELRY WARDROBE

By now your jewelry wardrobe should be in good shape. You've had the pieces repaired that were broken and unusable, and you've traded some of your unflattering pieces for "new-to-you" and flattering pieces. It's time to inventory, to find out what your next purchases should be.

The inventory sheet will show your past preferences, point out what's missing in your collection, and also provide a record for insurance purposes.

The following chart is designed to help you with this inventory. To use it, organize your jewelry items by categories: earrings, rings, bracelets, necklaces, pins, and pendants and then list them in the appropriate columns. With the chart filled in, you can tell at a glance what's in your jewelry wardrobe, so you can select pieces for wearing with ease and confidence. It also helps you see what your past preferences have been. But the foremost purpose of this chart is to enable you to spot the gaps and spaces in your entire collection and to plan logically for your future jewelry purchases.

Putting together a workable jewelry wardrobe today can be an expensive and time-consuming proposition. One of the keys to doing it well (and also within your budget) is to tag the most important pieces you now have and plan to build on them. One important benefit to be gained by inventorying your jewelry is to identify these essential pieces. On your chart you can mark these with a simple star, as is shown in the sample chart, or some other identifying mark.

If you have an important piece of jewelry, it can be a cornerstone of your jewelry collection.

And there is a bonus in doing this inventory. Many American women have a sizeable investment in their jewelry wardrobe. Filling out this inventory and keeping it up to date by adding your future purchases will enable you to use it for insurance appraisals and for police reports in the event your jewelry is ever stolen.

When you begin filling in the chart, describe each piece and note the type material used in making it (for example, gold filled, sterling silver, rhinestones). At the end of the inventory chart, there are several spaces for you to make a list of future purchases. Prioritizing these purchases takes time, thought, and planning now. But it can save you money in the long run. This list focuses your purchases—and by keeping these pieces in mind, you may even catch them on sale!

SAMPLE JEWELRY WARDROBE WORKSHEET

EARRINGS

Description	Color and Material		Look		Value	Insured?
	warm tone	cool tone	Dramatic Classic	Romantic Natural		
#1. gold button clips	14K. g.f.		Classic		$50	
#2. diamond earstuds		diamonds & platinum	Classic		$5000	✓
3. large bronze clips	bronze		Dramatic		$15	
4. filigree hoops		sterling silver	Romantic		$35	

SAMPLE JEWELRY SHOPPING LIST

Jewelry Piece Needed	Material	Look	To Go With
1. round earrings	gold-filled	Classic	dome ring & chain
2. choker beads	wood	Natural	2 wooden bangles

EARRING WORKSHEET

Description	Color and Material		Look		Value	Insured?
	warm tone	cool tone	Dramatic Classic			
			Romantic Natural			

EARRING SHOPPING LIST

Piece Needed	Material	Look	To Go With

BRACELET WORKSHEET

Description	Color and Material		Look		Value	Insured?
	warm tone	cool tone	Dramatic Romantic	Classic Natural		

_____

_____

_____

_____

_____

_____

_____

_____

_____

BRACELET SHOPPING LIST

Piece Needed	Material	Look	To Go With

_____

_____

_____

_____

_____

RING WORKSHEET

Description	Color and Material		Look		Value	Insured?
	warm tone	cool tone	Dramatic Romantic	Classic Natural		

_____

_____

_____

_____

_____

_____

_____

_____

_____

RING SHOPPING LIST

Piece Needed	Material	Look	To Go With

_____

_____

_____

_____

_____

_____

NECKLACE AND PENDANT WORKSHEET

Description	Color and Material		Look		Value	Insured?
	warm tone	cool tone	Dramatic Classic			
			Romantic Natural			

_____

_____

_____

_____

_____

_____

_____

_____

_____

_____

NECKLACE AND PENDANT SHOPPING LIST

Piece Needed	Material	Look	To Go With

_____

_____

_____

_____

_____

_____

PIN WORKSHEET

Description	Color and Material		Look		Value	Insured?
	warm tone	cool tone	Dramatic	Classic		
			Romantic	Natural		

_____

_____

_____

_____

_____

_____

_____

_____

_____

PIN SHOPPING LIST

Piece Needed	Material	Look	To Go With

_____

_____

_____

_____

_____

_____

When planning ahead and budgeting for new purchases, it helps to match the purchases to your lifestyle and priorities. Do you need jewelry that goes from 9–5? Pieces for formal occasions? Perhaps you lead a life that calls for a wide variety of jewelry.

How often you wear a piece of jewelry and how long you expect to keep it influences the price you should pay for the piece. A pair of earrings bought on sale may seem like a bargain, but if they fall apart or go out of style after only a couple of wearings, they're not. Likewise, a matched gemstone set bought especially for a cocktail party may seem just right. But if they're worn only a few times, they can turn out to be an expensive purchase. On the other hand, if the gemstone pieces are worn a few times a year over a lifetime, they may be the best jewelry bargain you ever got.

The following is a formula designed to help you compute the cost of your jewelry *per wearing* on a yearly basis. To see how it works, take the example of a professional woman who has $150 in her budget for jewelry. If she buys a gold bangle with this money and wears it to work regularly, its cost per wearing per year can be figured using the formula:

ORIGINAL COST / NUMBER OF TIMES WORN = COST PER WEARING

For example, the gold bangle's cost per wearing would be figured:

PIECE OF JEWELRY	ORIGINAL COST	AVERAGE TIMES WORN	COST PER WEARING (times/cost)
gold bangle	$150	3 days a week = 156	96¢

However, this same woman could decide that she needs a gemstone piece that she can wear to special occasions she attends after work hours. If the same woman used her money to buy a diamond drop, the cost per wearing would be:

PIECE OF JEWELRY	ORIGINAL COST	AVERAGE TIMES WORN	COST PER WEARING (times/cost)
diamond drop	$150	15 times total	$10

This formula is meant only as a guide to help you figure out the value of a piece of jewelry according to the number of times you wear it. If those occasions when you wear the diamond pendant are more important to you, then you will be wiser to spend your money on it. Only you know the impact of the occasion and the right jewelry to wear for it.

Once you decide to buy, take time to try on the pieces you're considering. You try on blouses, slacks, suits, and dresses to find the right size, color, and fit. So don't hesitate to try on rings, pins, bracelets, and earrings. And don't be rushed into a decision by an eager salesperson. You're the one who knows the right jewelry for you.

There's only one thing left — how to care for the jewelry now that you have it!

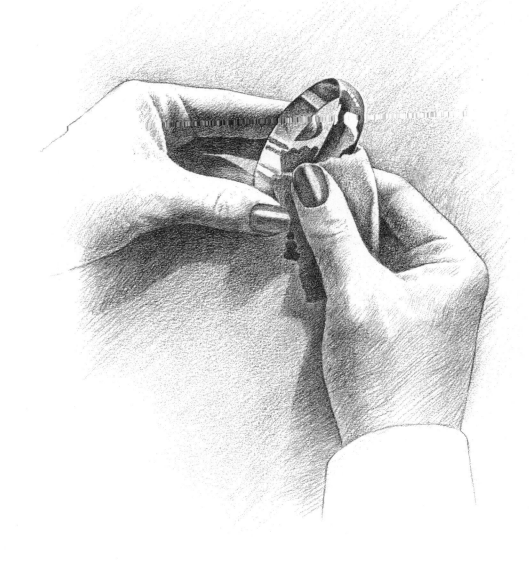

Part
III

Caring for Your Jewelry

10 *The Care and Cleaning of Your Jewelry*

To clean her jewelry, a woman bought a home ultrasonic jewelry cleaner. Happy with her purchase, she plopped a few pieces, including an emerald ring, into the machine and turned it on, returning a few minutes later to see how they looked. While the 14-karat gold earrings looked great, to her horror she found the emerald had shattered into small fragments. It was ruined forever.

Unfortunately, disaster stories like these are common. One little mistake can destroy a gemstone, pit a metal, or peel the layering from plated jewelry. Whether the jewelry is fine or costume, it is a delicate creation and subject to damage with careless action. As the story about the emerald ring points out, it's essential to know how to clean your jewelry.

Yet, all too often jewelry is sold without care and cleaning instructions. It's ironic that if you go shopping and buy a $20 blouse and a $2,000 emerald ring, the blouse would most likely come with more care and cleaning instructions than would the emerald.

Proper care and cleaning of your jewelry can enhance both the jewelry and you. Scratched bracelets and dirty diamonds do not flatter you. Neither do strands of pearls with frayed strings, nor kinked chains. Properly cleaned and cared for, your jewelry will look good on you when it is new and also give you a lifetime of wearing pleasure.

CLEANING

Modern technological advances have added new, improved methods of cleaning jewelry (ultrasonic waves) to the old tried-and-true methods (the toothbrush and soapy water). In general, there are six methods you can use to clean your jewelry: steam cleaning, ultrasonic, boiling, commercial chemical solutions, soapy water and a soft brush, and wiping with a soft cloth. Only one, the last one, can be used on any piece of jewelry without fear of damage. Of the other five, some provide sparkling results when used on certain materials or gemstones. But beware! Not all methods work on all types of jewelry. For example, the ultrasonic brings fire and brilliance back to a dirty diamond but brings disaster to emeralds. The cleaning process that is right for each piece of your jewelry depends on the materials and the type and quality of workmanship that went into making the piece.

Steam-cleaning Machines

Machines that use steam to clean jewelry operate a bit like a pressure cooker or a steam locomotive. They release a quick burst of hot steam that blows away dirt that has built up on a piece of jewelry. The steam loosens the particles, and the force of the burst blows them away. This is an extremely effective method of cleaning — for the right pieces of jewelry.

Unfortunately, this same hard blast of steam can force the dirt into any crack on a gemstone's surface instead of blowing it away. If used on costume jewelry set with artificial "stones" or poorly set gemstone jewelry, it can loosen the gemstones in their setting. The heat used in the process can also melt plastic pieces. However, most steam cleaners are too expensive for home use and are generally found only in jewelry stores.

Ultrasonic Bath

An ultrasonic cleaner sends high-frequency sound waves through a solution of soapy water. The sound waves cause the solution to vibrate and wash back and forth across the immersed piece. The motion of the water loosens and washes away any dirt particles or oil build-up. This is a great method for cleaning metals and tough gemstones, but, as you have seen, it wreaks havoc on more delicate gemstones.

Ultrasonic cleaners work well on all precious metal jewelry — karat, sterling, or filled. Remember to keep the bath solution one of mild soap and water because some cleaning solvents attack silver.

Costume jewelry pieces generally do not hold up under ultrasonic cleaning. They are usually made with less durable materials, their links and prongs are weaker, and often they are set with stones that have been glued in place.

Boiling

Boiling is a home remedy for cleaning jewelry with stubborn problems. Jewelry pieces are immersed in boiling soapy water, and the boiling action and detergent work to loosen the dirt. Although quite effective, this is an extremely risky method of cleaning. Boiling can shatter soft or fragile gemstones. Costume jewelry is too delicate to even attempt cleaning it by this method.

Compounding the stress of the high temperatures of this method is the fact that the jewelry is often taken directly from the boiling water and rinsed under a stream of cold tap water. This causes a quick and drastic change of temperature that can crack or shatter gemstones. Boiling should be considered hazardous for almost all jewelry pieces.

Cleaning Solutions and Pastes

Many times you are given a commercial jewelry cleaning solution when you purchase a piece of jewelry. This solution is safe to use in most cases, but if it contains ammonia, it can attack cultured pearls and many of the materials used in costume jewelry. In addition, any solution containing bleach can pit gold alloys.

Liquid or paste polishes designed especially for cleaning metals like brass, bronze, and silver are readily available and clean these metals effectively. However, if you are cleaning a mixed metal piece, be sure to tape off any of the space age metals (titanium, niobium, or tantalum) because metal polishes designed to clean brass, copper, or silver attack these newer metals. Be sure to avoid using any polish or abrasive on plated or filled metals. They rub off the thin outer layer of precious metal.

Plastics, which scratch easily, can be polished with car polish, then buffed to a high polish with a piece of soft cloth.

Mild, Soapy Water and a Soft Brush

Most jewelry responds well to this gentle cleaning method. Remember to use a mild detergent mixed with water—a few drops in a little warm water. Don't soak pearl strands or any pieces made with rhinestones. When you use this method to clean pieces set with stones, be sure to plug the sink to catch any loosened stones.

Cloths

Some of the materials that go into making jewelry are so soft and delicate they can only be cleaned by using a soft cloth. Generally, most inexpensive costume jewelry should be cleaned this way. Older costume pieces are especially frail and vulnerable to breaking because of age.

There are several types of treated polishing cloths available on the market today. These have been specially treated with chemicals that help remove dirt and oil from precious metal jewelry and also the tarnish that forms on silver. Because these cloths are soft, they are excellent to use on filled or plated pieces of both gold and silver. However, for costume jewelry and less durable gemstones, a soft, *untreated* cloth, like an old rag, is the best choice.

Cleaning Gemstones

You can never make a mistake in cleaning your gemstone jewelry by wiping it with a clean, soft, untreated cloth. But, of the other five methods of cleaning, some are appropriate only for certain gemstones. To clean each of your gemstone pieces safely,

GEMSTONE CLEANING METHODS

Gemstone	Toughness	Stable under cleaning by:					
		steam	ultra sonic	boil	cleaners	soap	untreated cloth
Diamond	good	yes	yes	yes	yes	yes	yes
Ruby	excellent	yes	yes	no	yes	yes	yes
Sapphire	excellent	yes	yes	no	yes	yes	yes
Emerald	poor	no	no	no	no	yes	yes
Pearl	poor	no	no	no	no	no	yes
Alexandrite	excellent	yes	yes	no	yes	yes	yes
Amber	poor	no	no	no	no	no	yes
Amethyst	good	no	no	no	yes	yes	yes
Aquamarine	fair	no	no	no	yes	yes	yes
Citrine	good	no	no	no	yes	yes	yes
Coral	fair	no	no	no	no	yes	yes
Garnet	good	no	no	no	yes	yes	yes
Iolite	poor	no	no	no	no	no	yes
Jade	excellent	yes	no	yes	no	yes	yes
Kunzite	poor	no	no	no	yes	yes	yes
Lapis Lazuli	fair	no	no	no	yes	yes	yes
Opal	poor	no	no	no	no	no	yes
Peridot	poor	no	no	no	no	no	yes
Spinel	good	yes	yes	no	yes	yes	yes
Tanzanite	poor	no	no	no	no	yes	yes
Topaz	poor	no	no	no	no	yes	yes
Tourmaline	good	no	no	no	yes	yes	yes
Turquoise	good	no	no	no	no	yes	yes
Zircon	fair	yes	yes	no	yes	yes	yes

first be sure you know exactly what the stone is and what condition it is in. Visually inspect it for any chips or cracks. If you are in doubt, have a qualified jeweler give you advice. The opposite chart lists the twenty-five gemstones described in detail in Chapter Seven and the cleaning processes safe for each.

CARE

I f one set of instructions came with all jewelry, it would read "Handle with Care!" There are three important guidelines to follow in caring for your jewelry: separate it, give it periodic checkups, and don't wear it during vigorous activity.

Three guidelines for caring for your jewelry are:

1) separate it
2) have it checked once a year
3) take it off during vigorous physical activity.

Most jewelry comes packaged in soft sacks, boxes, or wrapped in tissue paper. There is a good reason for this individual packaging: jewelry is supposed to rest against your body, not other pieces of jewelry.

When something hard, such as a diamond or glass, rubs against something soft, such as gold, pearls, or plastic, the softer materials come out the losers. That's why it is a poor idea to toss your rhinestone ear clips in the bottom of your jewelry box right next to your string of cultured pearls or your silver bangle. Separating your jewelry in individual boxes, bags, or the compartments of your jewelry box will help it to last a lifetime.

So will periodic checkups. Most cars get regular checkups; preventive maintenance on engines and transmission often avoids major disasters. So, too, does a periodic maintenance check of your jewelry, especially your fine gemstone jewelry, help avoid irretrievable losses. A jeweler's inspection can reveal loose mountings, cracked stones, and unreliable clasps. Your important and valuable pieces of jewelry should be checked once a year. In particular, pearls should be taken into your jeweler at least this often to check for fraying of the silk strand used to string them.

Finally, no jewelry holds up well under hard physical activity. Whether you are doing heavy chores, playing a set of tennis, or taking a dip in a chlorinated pool, your jewelry isn't strong enough to go with you. While normal wear gives your jewelry minute scratches that turn into a beautiful, soft patina, hard blows do not. Removing all jewelry before beginning physical activities can help prevent a disappointing damage or loss later.

GLOSSARY OF JEWELRY TERMS

Alloy—A mixture of two or more metals. Metals are alloyed by weight. For example, 100 ounces of sterling silver is 92.5 ounces silver/7.5 ounces copper.

Aluminum—A silver-colored metal, known for its lightness, malleability, and resistance to oxidation.

Art Deco—A style fashionable in the 1920s and 1930s. Art Deco jewelry featured abstract designs and geometric patterns.

Art Nouveau—A style of the 1890s and early 1900s emphasizing free-flowing, curving lines with asymmetrical natural motifs. For example, intertwining floral patterns, butterflies and dragonflies, and delicate female faces were commonly used in Art Nouveau jewelry.

Asterism—The starlike reflection of white lines present in some gemstones. Asterism is most prevalent in rubies and sapphires.

Bangle Bracelet—A nonflexible type of bracelet that slips easily over the hand.

Baroque Pearl—A large, irregularly shaped pearl.

Base Metal—Any nonprecious metal. In the jewelry industry, copper, zinc, brass, lead, and antimony are usually referred to as the base metals.

Bezel Setting — A type of setting in which the rim holds the stone, completely surrounding the gem. Bezels can be molded into any shape to fit the stone, such as straight edges or scalloped.

Biwa Pearl — A variety of cultured pearls produced in fresh water. Biwa pearls come in a variety of colors and are often bleached to a bright white. They are usually irregular in shape.

Brass — An alloy of copper and zinc. The proportions are variable. Most common alloys in jewelry-making are between 80 and 90 percent copper and 10 to 20 percent zinc.

Brilliant Cut — A gemstone cut generally used for diamonds.

Bronze — An alloy containing copper and tin and other elements such as phosphorus, aluminum, and silicon. Several modern copper alloys are called bronzes because they look like bronze even though they do not contain tin. For example, commercial bronze is 90 percent copper and 10 percent zinc.

Cabochon — A gemstone cut that features a smooth, rounded surface.

Carat — A measure of weight used for gemstones, equal to 200 milligrams or $\frac{1}{5}$ gram.

Casting — The process of forming an object by pouring molten metal into a hollow mold.

Channel Setting—A type of setting in which the gemstones are set into a channel or single row, with no metal or very thin strips separating them.

Charm—A small, decorative article worn suspended from a bracelet. A charm is usually part of a collection of such objects.

Charm Bracelet—A popular type of bracelet from which a variety of decorative charms are hung.

Choker—A short necklace that fits closely around the neck, 14 to 16 inches long.

Clarity—A term used to define the clearness of a gemstone or absence of internal flaws.

Coin Silver—90 percent (90/100) fine silver and 10 percent copper. The same alloy was used for U.S. silver coins before 1966. Since 1966, U.S. dimes, quarters, and half dollars are made from two sheets of nickel with a center of copper. They contain no silver.

Copper—A light, inexpensive, malleable metal. This reddish-brown metal looks like pink gold and has the same properties as brass.

Costume Jewelry—Jewelry made of moderately priced to inexpensively priced materials. Originally, costume jewelry was made for a certain type of costume.

Cuff Bracelet—A nonflexible type bracelet, made in the form of a wide cylindrical band, featuring either an open back or a hinge. Cuffs slip over the wrist and fit tighter than bangles.

Cultured Pearl — A type of pearl that is created within a mollusk by manually inserting an irritant into the shell. This becomes the nucleus of the pearl and is surrounded by layers of nacre.

Cut — The shape of a stone when changed from a rough stone to a gem.

Danish Silver — Silverware made in Denmark is $830/1000$ fine silver if made to minimum Danish standards and $925/1000$ fine silver if made for export.

Die Striking — Essentially, the same method used by ancient Greeks to make their coins. A die-struck object is produced by striking metal on one or between two dies. The stamping hammer forces the metal, under tremendous pressure, into every crevice of the die cavity and the metal forms into the shape of the die cavity. "Coining" is a term sometimes used to refer to this process.

Doublet — A composite stone made of two layers fused together, appearing as a whole natural stone.

Ear Clip — A type of earring that is secured to the ear lobe by a hinged support.

Ear Hook — A type of earring in which a slender loop of wire slips through the ear lobe.

Ear Stud — A type of earring consisting of a front part that fits through the ear lobe and connects to the back part, called a clutch, behind the lobe. When worn, only the front part is seen.

Earring—An ear ornament, worn at the ear either by means of a wire or thin hoop passing through a hole pierced in the lobe of the ear, or fastened with a screw or clip.

Electroplating—A process using electrical current to coat objects with a thin layer of metal.

Emerald Cut—A gemstone cut generally used for a diamond or an emerald. The stone is cut into a square or rectangular shape with step cut sides.

Engraving—The process of cutting a design on a hard surface (metal, stone, or wood) with a sharp instrument.

Facet—Any of the small, polished plane surfaces of a gemstone.

Fancies—Diamonds that are naturally colored and extremely rare.

Filigree—A style of intertwining strands of gold or silver wire.

Fine Gold—99.9 percent gold or higher; contains no alloy material. Fine gold is 24K gold.

Fine Silver—Commercially pure silver, 99.9 percent fine or higher, that contains no alloy material.

Flexible—See LINK BRACELET.

German Silver—A composition of nickel, copper, and zinc containing no silver whatsoever.

Gilding—The process of covering silver, base metal, or some other substance (e.g., wood) with a thin layer of gold, either pure gold or a gold alloy.

Gold—A heavy, precious metal. Gold is the most popular jewelry metal today.

Gold Filled—A process by which a layer of at least 10K gold has been mechanically bonded to a base metal. This layer must constitute at least 1/20 of the total weight of the metal in the piece.

Gold Leaf—Developed by the Egyptians, this dwindling craft goes back 6,500 years. Skilled gold-beaters hammered gold sheets separated by ox membranes into extremely thin sheets. Gold leaf is used for decorative purposes, including picture frames, signs, book edges, and ornaments.

Gold Plate—See ELECTROPLATING.

Gold Washed—Term used for a gold electroplate that is thinner than 7/1,000,000 of an inch of fine gold. It is also known as "gold-flashed."

Heavy Gold Electroplate—The term for electroplating of gold or gold alloy of a minimum 10K fineness, with a minimum thickness of 100 millionths of an inch of fine gold.

Imitation Gemstone—An artificial stone used to imitate the appearance of a natural gemstone. Such copies have totally different physical and chemical characteristics than a natural gemstone.

Inclusion—Any foreign matter that is enclosed within a mineral or crystal.

Jewelry—Any decorative piece consisting of metal, gemstones, or certain organic materials intended to be worn by the person for adornment or pleasure.

K—Stands for karat.

Karat—A measure of fineness equal to $\frac{1}{24}$ part by weight of the metallic element gold in an alloy. Fine or pure gold is 24 karats. Example: if an article is made of 18K gold, it is 18 parts pure gold and 6 parts other metal by weight, or 75 percent gold.

Karat Gold—In the United States, a gold alloy of not less than 10K fineness. The term is synonymous with "real gold" when referring to fine jewelry.

Link Bracelet—A type of flexible bracelet made up of a series of links.

Marquise Cut—A type of cut in the shape of a boat or a pointed oval, which features 56 facets.

Matinee—A strand of pearls or length of necklace approximately 20 to 24 inches long.

Matrix—The weblike coloring in a gemstone such as a turquoise.

Mexican Silver — A name given to the silver used by many Mexican and American Indian craftsmen. Its silver content is generally above 90 percent, some as much as 99 percent, although there is no guarantee of the percentage of silver.

Mohs Scale — A scale for measuring the hardness of a mineral or other hard substance, developed in 1812 by Austrian Friedrich Mohs. Mohs took ten well-known minerals and assigned them numbers according to their hardness. The minerals are 1) talc; 2) gypsum; 3) calcite; 4) fluorspar; 5) apatite; 6) orthoclase; 7) quartz; 8) topaz; 9) sapphire; 10) diamond. Intervals between the minerals are indicated by fractions.

Nickel — A hard, silver-white metal, used in alloys and plating.

Nickel Silver — An alloy so called because of some color resemblance to silver. In reality, it is a composition of nickel, copper, and zinc. Nickel silver contains no silver and is primarily used in costume jewelry.

Niobium — A rare, malleable space-age metal. Most people have no allergic reaction to it.

Opaque — Does not permit light to pass through.

Opera — A strand of pearls or length of necklace approximately 28 to 30 inches long.

Pave Setting — A jewelry setting in which small gems are placed close together.

Pear Shaped—A type of gemstone cut, sometimes called "drop shaped."

Pendant—An ornament suspended from a neck chain or necklace.

Pewter—A fairly soft alloy with a high proportion of tin.

Platinum—A steel-gray, easy-to-form precious metal that is very resistant to corrosion.

Point—A weight measurement used for stones less than one carat (one carat = 100 points).

Precious Metals—Gold, silver, and the six metals of platinum gold are also called the noble or precious metals. These metals are valued above others because of chemical and physical properties such as resistance to corrosion, hardness, strength, and beauty, and also because they are relatively rare or expensive.

Princess—A strand of pearls or length of necklace approximately 18 inches long.

Rhinestone—A colorless, artificial gem often cut as an imitation of a diamond.

Rolled Gold Plate—Same as gold-filled except the quantity of karat gold is less than $1/20$ of the total metal weight. It must be identified with a fraction indicating the quantity of gold (e.g., $1/40$ 12K R.G.P.).

Rope—A strand of pearls or length of necklace approximately 40 inches long.

Sautoir — See ROPE.

Seed Pearl — A very small round pearl, often irregular, that weighs less than one-quarter of a grain.

Silver — A white precious metal. Silver is extremely malleable and combines well with other metals.

Solid Gold — A term that some would reserve for fine or 24K gold because it contains no other metals (alloys); however, in 1967 the Federal Trade Commission held that "solid gold" may be used to describe articles that do not have a hollow center and are at least 10K or finer alloy, such as 14K or 18K.

Sterling Silver — 92½ percent fine silver and 7½ percent copper.

Surgical Steel — A light, inexpensive metal, generally used for earwires and hypo-allergenic jewelry.

Synthetic Gemstone — A man-made stone that has the same appearance, chemical composition, and physical characteristics as a natural gemstone.

Tantalum — A rare, steel-blue metal which can be given beautiful colors by torches or electrolysis.

Tiffany Setting — A type of setting in which the stone is secured by six prongs.

Titanium — A dark gray, hard, but lightweight metal. It is difficult to work with and cannot be soldered. Most people have no allergic reaction to it.

Translucent — Letting light pass through, but in a diffused manner so that objects behind cannot be seen distinctly.

Transparent — Permitting light rays without diffusion so that objects behind can be seen distinctly.

Triplet — A composite stone made of three layers — two layers of stone and a middle layer of colored cement — which enhances the color of the whole stone.

Vermeil — Gold-electroplating over a sterling silver base.

PURSE-SIZE JEWELRY REFERENCE GUIDE

Now that you are familiar with the guidelines for buying and wearing the right jewelry for you, you may want to have a purse-size jewelry reference guide to take with you when you shop.

Each reference guide contains information about the jewelry that best suits your hands, face and personality as well as quick reminders of jewelry terms commonly encountered when shopping, traditional birthstones, and the content of precious metals.

Included with this handy guide is a plastic ring sizer and a year's subscription to catalogs featuring the most popular designs of James Avery. To order, send $2.00 (which includes shipping and handling) to the address below or call toll free.

The Right Jewelry Reference Guide
James Avery Craftsman, Inc.
P.O. Box 1367, Dept. RJ
Kerrville, TX 78029
1-800-531-7198
1-800-292-7059 (in Texas)